The Twenty-Eighth Regiment Iowa Volunteer Infantry

E. E. Blake

Camp Pope
2021

Originally published 1896 by the Union Press,
Belle Plaine, Iowa

New Materials Copyright © 2021
by Camp Pope Publishing

ISBN: 978-1-929919-92-5

FOREWORD
BY ROXANA CURRIE

Ephraim Blake enlisted in the Army at Marengo, Iowa, August 15, 1862. The 20-year-old farmer was 5'10" and fair, with hazel eyes and auburn hair. The federal government was paying a bounty to enlistees to avoid as long as possible the need for a draft. Some states or even townships added to that bonus. Blake was paid a $25 bounty with a $2.00 premium for giving the next three years of his life to the preservation of the Union.

Born in Monroe County, Ohio, in 1842, he had come to Iowa with his parents, Jason and Catherine Blake, at the age of nine. The family settled near Buckeye, Iowa, in Benton County.

He farmed with his father until Abraham Lincoln's call for 300,000 new volunteers in 1862. The 28th Iowa Volunteers were organized from Benton, Tama, Poweshiek, Iowa, Jasper, and Johnson counties. They were mustered into the service of the United States on October 10th at Camp Pope, near Iowa City.

Blake's biographical sketch in *Portrait and Biographical Album of Benton County, Iowa*, published in 1887, says,

> As a private in Co. G, 28th Iowa Vol. Inf., [he] served three years in the war of the Rebellion. He was with Grant at Vicksburg, and with Banks up Red River,

E. E. Blake

where he was captured but made his escape. He was with Sheridan in the Shenandoah Valley campaigns. He saw three years of active service without missing a day's duty or a single ration when he could get it.[1]

Blake writes in long, rambling sentences, but with interesting detail about the various experiences three years as a soldier entailed. Of course he recounts endless marches and pitched battles. Of course there were beloved and not so beloved commanding officers. There were experiences of worn out clothes nearly falling off the body, and there were spit and polish parades. There were winter quarters in mountainous areas, which was quite a new experience for an Iowa boy. At least mountains had plenty of wood for fires. There were many many wet swamps and river crossings. Surprisingly, his regiment took two ocean-going boat trips.

When it was over, Blake came home to Iowa, spending another two years on his father's farm. He married Emma Swezey July 31, 1867, and their first daughter, Olive was born. The little family then moved to LeMars, Iowa. Blake studied law there, reading with a local lawyer as was the practice then. In 1872 he was elected to the first of three terms of clerk of court in Plymouth County. Three more daughters were born in LeMars.

---

1. *Portrait and Biographical Album of Benton County, Iowa* (Chicago: Chapman Bros., 1887), 277.

THE 28TH IOWA INFANTRY

Scandal seems to have followed Blake during his time in LeMars. Local newspapers recount more than one episode of unfaithfulness, not suited to an elected official. In February of 1878 the *LeMars Iowa Liberal* featured Blake in a front page story which concludes,

> If this were his first escapade of this kind, there might be room for pity and commiseration, but having just emerged from under the cloud of a disgraceful transaction it seems to us that he deserves nought but the severest condemnation. A county officer given to acts such as have been indulged in by Blake, is a disgrace to the people who elected and who support him, and unless a radical change in his conduct is made at once, he must be removed. Such flagrant violations of decency cannot longer be tolerated.

The family returned to Benton County, settling in Belle Plaine around 1879. Their youngest daughter, Libbie, was born there in 1885. Eight children were born to the couple; only four daughters survived to adulthood.

Only glimpses of Blake's life in Belle Plaine survive. He worked as a night clerk at the Burley House and wrote early history articles for the *Belle Plaine Union* newspaper. Ephraim began working for the Chicago and North Western Railway, starting at the bottom and working his way up to manager of the railroad's company store. In 1895 he was justice of the peace in Belle Plaine.

The *Waterloo Courier* noted in an April 1896 article that "E. E. Blake, of Belle Plaine, is writing a history of the 28th Iowa, which he expects to have ready for the reunion of that regiment at that place July 3 and 4."

Blake mentions the process in the introduction to his book. "I had no thought that I should ever do so and that I did is as great a surprise to myself as it will be to my comrades," he writes. "It was an accident, and was brought about by the editor of the *Union*, Fred W. Browne, requesting a personal reminiscence of the war for publication for the purpose of interesting the people at Belle Plaine, Iowa, in the reunion of the regiment." The Union Press of Belle Plaine became the publisher when the reminiscence turned into a book.

In 1898 Blake was divorced from his first wife, Emma. In 1900 Emma took her youngest daughter, Libbie, to Colorado, "in search of a more agreeable climate."[2] His daughter Libbie was married in Colorado in 1905, and Emma remained there until her death in 1911.

The *Muscatine Evening Journal* mentions Blake in 1900 as the editor of the *Belle Plaine Herald*.

In 1903 Blake and widow Bessie Watts Gildroy were married by the mayor of Belle Plaine. It's unclear where the couple settled.

---

2. *Muscatine Evening Journal*, April 27, 1900.

THE 28TH IOWA INFANTRY

In 1906 Blake's daughter, Grace, moved with her husband Ed Fanske to Pierce, Nebraska. They opened a jewelry store, which served the community through a second generation until 1933. An article in the May 25, 1916, *Pierce County Leader* states, "Mr. and Mrs. E. E. Blake arrived in the city Saturday from Montana, and will make their home with their daughter."

That is where Blake died in November 1919 at the age of 77. The old soldier was laid to rest in Prospect View Cemetery in Pierce, Nebraska.

Roxana Currie is a popular historian in Polk County, Iowa, who has written often about local history and the service of Polk County men in the Civil War.

E. E. Blake

PUBLISHER'S NOTE

Blake's history of the 28th Iowa Infantry contains a 55-page Field and Staff Roster, which has not been included in this reprint. That appendix is unfortunately incomplete and full of errors. Anyone wishing to find information on members of the 28th Iowa Infantry volunteers can access it in the *Roster and Records of Iowa Soldiers in the War of the Rebellion* (http://iagenweb.org/civilwar/books/logan/mil512.htm) or the National Park Service's Soldiers and Sailors Database (https://www.nps.gov/civilwar/soldiers-and-sailors-database.htm).

Blake's text is reprinted here exactly as he wrote it, including misspellings, incorrect grammar and sentence structure, and inconsistent styling, with only minimal corrections and additions to clarify contexts.

A SUCCINCT HISTORY

OF THE

28th Iowa Volunteer Infantry.

From Date of Muster Into Service, October 10th, 1862, at Iowa City, Iowa, to its Final Muster Out, August 13th, 1865, at Davenport, Iowa.

BY E. E. BLAKE,
Private, Co. G.

Covering Every March, Skirmish and Battle Throughout the Sieges of Vicksburg, Jackson, Teche and Red River Expeditions, The Shenandoah Valley Campaign, 1864, and the trip to Savannah, New Berne and Augusta.

1896.
Belle Plaine, Iowa,
UNION PRESS.

To the
Mothers, Wives, Children and Descendants
of the Regiment,
this book
is Respectfully Dedicated by
E. E. Blake,
Private Company G

PREFACE

It was my good fortune to be born July 17, 1842, and attain to manhood's estate in time to enter the service and become a member of the gallant 28th Iowa, in the war of the rebellion. It was also my good fortune to follow the regiment through all of its marches, skirmishes, and battles without contracting disease, being seriously wounded, or killed in battle. When I entered the service I was just at the age when the mind is most easily impressed with sights and scenes that come under personal observation and being blessed with a retentive memory, the incidents connected with soldier life is as vivid today as they were in the days of the war. I have always hoped someone capable of writing a history of our service, would take up the task and give us a complete history in book form of our travels and conflicts during our three years of service; I had no thought that I should ever do so and that I did is as great a surprise to myself as it will be to my comrades. It was an accident and was brought about by the editor of the UNION, Fred W. Browne, requesting a personal reminiscence of the war for publication for the purpose of interesting the people at Belle Plaine, Ia., in the reunion of the regiment July 3d and 4th, 1896. I began the story with our entry into the service in Aug. 1862. I began "fighting them over again" and sights and scenes began crowding upon me and I continued the story (aided in data by Chaplain Simmon's history of the

E. E. Blake

regiment) and the result is a simple narrative of the regiment's travels, skirmishes, battles and hardships which being put in book form I shall call a history. It is not all I could desire, yet is the best I could do in the time I have devoted to the work, that it is wanting in style and composition I am ready to admit, but it tells of our services and may be of value to some carping critic who may not be satisfied and undertake to write one himself, if not to others. In this my first and last attempt to write a book for the multitude to read, there are recorded many incidents of interest to the old veterans of the regiment, there are thousands of other incidents that ought to be included, there were many incidents of personal daring by officers and men that I should have been glad to mention but not having time to gather and group them in their proper place with any degree of satisfaction I have avoided personal mention except in a general way, and confined my narrative to the regiment as a regiment, only adding a little spice to make it readable.

That it may in some measure help to perpetuate the noble deeds, the heroic service and terrible sacrifices of the members of the brave old 28th Iowa and keep their memories fresh and green in the minds of our children and those that follow them, is the only hope of the author. If it does this then I am satisfied.

E. E. Blake
Private of Co. G.

The 28th Iowa Infantry

A Brief History of the Movements of this Noble Iowa Regiment

Written by E. E. Blake, of Company G.

In the early spring time of the year 1861, when Belle Plaine was just pecking at the shell of time for an entrance on her future progress as a city, there came vibrating over the peaceful prairies the boom of the first gun fired in the great war of the rebellion, followed by a call by the president for volunteers to go out and fight for the nation's life and the old flag.

At that time this country was but sparsely settled, yet the call was heard by many in the early days of the war and hundreds went forth to battle, thinking it would not take many months to crush out the rebellion. A year passed, many hard battles had been fought and many who went out from this section of the state had sickened and died, or fallen in battle, while others languished in hospital and prison pens.

Then it was, President Lincoln made another call for

300,000 more, and recruiting offices were opened for others still to follow.

It was under this call the 28th Iowa, as gallant a regiment as ever marched to the beat of drums, was organized.

The regiment was rendezvoused at Camp Pope, Iowa City, in mustard into the United States service by H. B. Hendershott, October 10, 1862. It was composed of 956 men rank and file, commanded by Colonel William E. Miller. Companies A, B, C, D, F, G, H, and I, We're all made up in the county's compromising the Big 4 District, viz., Benton, Tama, Poweshiek and Iowa. Company K from Jasper and E from Johnson County. Ten companies of as brave boys as ever left good homes and warm firesides to fight for "Old Glory."

Boys who counted the cost before enlisting and knew their chances to fall in battle, die of disease, or starve in prison pen were great, but who loved their country and their country's flag well enough to face the hardships of the march, the hell of battle, the horror of the prison cell, and the deadly miasma among the swamps and lagoons of the South, and go bravely forth.

It is of the lives and services of the men of this regiment we wish to write, which will in some measure represent the lives and services of the 2,859,253 soldiers who went out to battle during the war on the Union side. After a camp life of two months occupied in drilling the different company and regimental drills, getting our schooling in the manual of arms, we were ordered south.

THE 28TH IOWA INFANTRY

On November 2, 1862, goodbyes were said to the many friends gathered to bid us God speed and we boarded cars for Davenport. Went into camp at Camp Herron, remaining one week waiting transportation, then took passage on the steamer *Hawkeye* for the South, reaching Helena, Arkansas, on the 20th of November, and were assigned to the First Brigade, Second Division, East Arkansas, and went into camp on the bank of the river above the town. Seven days afterward 300 of the regiment were ordered on an expedition to Oakland, Miss., under command of Brig. Gen. Hovey, for the purpose of making a diversion in favor of or reinforcing Gen. Grant then following the rebel General Price south from Holly Springs, Miss.

This was our first march and one long to be remembered. We were "Tender feet" then and like others before and many since, tried to carry all our possessions and pick up additional articles by the way, but a few miles traveled through mud and rain carrying an overloaded knapsack, 100 rounds of ammunition, gun and accoutrements and ten days rations, soon convinced us the less we carried the better we could march and the longer we would last, and ere many hours passed, knapsacks were emptied or abandoned. All superfluous articles cast away and the march continued.

Twenty miles a day through mud and rain with dried crackers and swamp water, was a change from the peaceful home and biscuits and butter for breakfast, we had left so recently, yet there was no complaining. We had come for war and hardships and expected it. Our trip was without incident until we reach Cold Water River crossing, where the Johns had a guard stationed. They had no knowledge of our near approach and were enjoying themselves, one was playing a violin, others dancing, some were up in the branches of the trees, when the advance guided by a faithful black pushed the nose of a six pounder through the brush and just as one fellow said "well about this time tomorrow night we may expect the cussed yanks." A six pound ball went crashing into a tree in their midst, and there was a rushing for safety. Our cavalry plunged into the river, swam their horses across, and gave chase, captured quite a number of longhaired fellows, who could cuss a yank with as much satisfaction as we could skin a shoat or pick a rooster captured on the march. It was here one of the boys in Company B, whose feet had become sore from the constant marching (having made 30 miles that day) concluded a good soaking in hot water would release them from pain. He waited until the rest had turned in then procured the company mess kettle and heating some water, proceeded to soap, soak and wash his dirty feet, afterwards washing out his dirty socks in the same soapy water. Now if he had emptied out the water and washed up the kettle, probably it might have been all right, but this he failed to do, and having stayed up later than the rest was not up with them in the morning to prevent what happened afterwards. His comrades waking earlier than he, seeing the camp kettle half full of water, built up their fire, put on the kettle put in their coffee and prepared the morning meal. After the coffee was ready, they sat down on the ground, as was the custom, dipped in their cups and began to drink. The first one to take a sup began to spit and sputter and cuss, wanting to know what in the thunder they had put in to give such skunky flavor to the coffee. Another followed adding his sulfurous remarks to the first, the third victim said the swamp water was worse than usual and by the time they all had a taste it was decided something must have died in the kettle the night before and the contents thereof was turned out to enrich the soil along the banks of the Cold Water. After the victims had learned the cause of the rotten smell of their morning beverage, there was some silent and very forcible language indulged in not very complementary to the poor fellow who had thoughtlessly increased the strength of their morning drink. After the circumstances had become known, the victims got many a jibe from the boys as they passed along. However they got their stomachs settled before the date passed and everything was serene—but not forgotten.

December 3rd the advance were charged on by some rebel cavalry near Oakland, and before they could get into a defensive position, the rebs captured one of our 6 pound guns, pulled General Washburn off his horse and very nearly carried him off, before they were repulsed. We were 4 miles in the rear, and were ordered up on double quick, but too late for service. That night we slept in a church in Oakland. After we had taken possession of the church, some women came and told us it had been used for smallpox hospital and we would all get the dreadful malady if we remained in it, thinking to scare us out, but the story did not work. We told them we had had it two or three times already and liked it, and they departed.

That night our cavalry and the Confederates were skirmishing all night, but five miles away, and from a prisoner captured, we learned General Price was near at hand, that Grant had abandoned his expedition south, and, feeling assured 600 infantry and a brigade of cavalry was not a sufficient force to oppose [General Sterling] Price's 15,000 men, we, by quick quiet marches sought safety on the other side of Cold Water River, where other troops were encamped.

The colored people had heard "De Linkum Sojer had done aribed," and thousands came flocking into this point, seeking freedom from slavery's chains. They held jollification meetings, preached, sang, prayed and shouted, because "De Year Ob Jubilee had come and De Linkum Sojer too." Poor fellows they had suffered long and patiently, who could blame them.

We lost one man on this expedition private William Hall of Company C, shot by a guerrilla, the first blood shed by the regiment for country and home.

This was our first war experience and a rough one. Only the beginning of what proved to be almost a daily occurrence for two and a half years to follow. It was on this trip that Fred Schaffer says he was out foraging and found a corn crib full of popcorn, he got off his "mewl" and tied him to the fence and set the corn on fire, and it went to popping and flying about, until the ground for rods was covered just like snow and Fred declares the mewl thought it was snow, and was shivering when he went to mount, and actually froze to death, compelling Fred to walk back to camp. Some way I have always doubted this story of Fred's.

Returning to Helena we went into camp, took up our share of the picket duty around over the backbone ridges around the town. Occasionally drilling by companies, regiments and brigades until January 11, 1863, when we started on an expedition up White River Arkansas Commanded by Gen. Gorman. The journey was by boat, the experience varied and exciting.

The White River is a narrow crooked stream, and at the time the expedition was under way, was swollen by the heavy rains until it overflowed its banks on the north side, and boats trying to make the turn of the numerous bends, would often leave the channel and go crashing out into the timber and underbrush, until stopped by coming in contact with a tree. Sometimes they would run between two trees and become wedged so tight it would require another boat to pull them out, as a result of those overland trips nearly all the boats had their smokestacks knocked off and were otherwise damaged.

Occasionally a bending branch would come sweeping back along the side of a boat and catch some unlucky soldier and pitch him into the cold water, to be fished out and put away under the boilers to dry. However on the 14th, we arrived at St. Charles, expecting to find opposition here, our regiment was unloaded with others, but the Confederates had left the town and we took possession of the vacated houses and proceeded to make ourselves comfortable as we could. It was here some of the 29th Wisconsin boys, in order to supply themselves with fresh meat, caught and killed an ancient William Goat. I have always wished they had taken him over into some other state to skin him, there was no staying in that town after they began ripping him up the belly. An Irishman said, "Be the powers of Moll Kelly the smell of a skoonk is not a patchin to the smell of the critter."

At 10 o'clock, contrary to expectations, we were ordered aboard the boats again, it was raining and snowing, the mud in the streets was anywhere from 4 to 12 inches deep, the night pitch dark until a thoughtful lover of light and warmth set a building on fire, then another, until our way was made plain and we marched onto the boats. There were several large ware houses standing along the landing. Our fleet of boats was tied up with their bows wedged in along the shore, fires were down and no steam up. Among the rest was the *Imperial*, a large lower river steamer loaded with ordinance stores. Someone not satisfied with the fire already kindled in the town set these warehouses on fire and soon the whole wharf was a roaring seething mass of flames and our boats all endangered, in fact the whole command was in great danger, for had our boats taken fire crowded as they were with troops, hundreds would have perished. It was only by the most heroic effort of the troops a general conflagration was averted. The *Imperial* was smoking hot. Had it took fire the exploding

THE 28TH IOWA INFANTRY

shells and immense amount of ammunition would have been disastrous. However by cutting the hawsers and letting our boats drift out into the stream and the free use of water, we escaped what for some time looked like a terrible disaster. Our gunboats having steam up came to our assistance piloting the transports to places of safety down the river. There were some narrow escapes from drowning, quite a number of the boys thinking to jump from one boat to another as they were drifting, not being able to calculate the distance went down into the cold dark water with a splash and a yelp for a rope. All were rescued and sent to a warm place by the boilers.

Next day we proceeded on our way up the river through a heavy snowstorm and in due time arrived at Duvall's Bluffs, where we captured two heavy siege guns and a few prisoners. Sherman having captured Arkansas Post we returned to Helena again, arriving on the 23rd of January at nine o'clock at night. Marched up to our old camp ground through mud, rain and cold to find every vestige of the comfortable quarters we had left on our departure, gone.

This expedition so barren in its results, cost the lives of many of our brave boys, constant exposure to rain and biting cold cramped up in our crowded condition on the decks of steamers with poor rations and adulterated coffee brought on disease to hundreds and ultimate death to many. Poor fellows. It is a sad sight to see hundreds sicken and die under circumstances like these but it was a part of our lot. From this time until April 11, 1863, we passed the time doing picket duty around the town often made exciting by frequent raids on the line by guerrillas. Wrestling with mumps, measles, smallpox and graybacks, and burying our comrades, who were daily passing away in camp in hospital.

These were the dark days of the rebellion. Our armies were being defeated in all the important engagements in the east, dissatisfaction because of the prosecution of the war was widespread among the Copperhead element of the Democrat Party in the North; disloyal fathers were writing loyal sons in the army to desert the old flag and go and assist the South. Disease and death were thinning our already depleted ranks, and a gloom thicker than the fog on the stagnant pools in the swamps of the South seemed to hang over us. Yet none faltered, through all the gloom they kept their eyes on the Stars & Stripes. "Old glory still waved." There was one thing that always brought relief to the members of the regiment while stationed at this godforsaken and never to be forgotten place. That was the picket duty. It was a relief to get away from the camp and hospital, the constant beat of the muffled drums and dead march, constant reminders that despite all our efforts to prevent, our ranks were daily being thinned by the many diseases prevalent in and about this fever breeding, pestilential hole. Our picket lines circled the town like a half moon, about a half-mile distant from the corporate limits. Most if not all the lines ran through the heavily wooded hills and hollows. These hills were high and steep with a narrow ridge, the hollows were narrow with barely room for a wagon road along the margin of the stream passing through them.

The woods were alive with hawks, owls, birds of many species; coons, chipmunks, gray squirrels and other small animals were plenty, so that night or day, we always had something to draw our minds away from the sufferings of camp life. Besides, the ever watchful guerrilla was always prowling around to get a whack at some luckless yank they might catch off his guard. They used every artifice to get near enough to our picket posts to kill and then get away. One night we heard a cow bell donging along down the side of the hill toward our post in the hollow, and at first we supposed it was a cow belonging to a man by the name of Underwood, who lived outside the lines and claimed to be loyal, cropping the grass along the slope. But when two loads of buckshot came swishing in among us and the rattle of the bell ceased, we began to understand the situation, that it was Underwood instead of his cow.

After that little experience it became dangerous for anyone or anything to approach our lines unless we were first apprised of their coming. A week or so afterwards a runaway slave approached the lines one dark night. The boys heard him coming down the hillside through the underbrush and supposing it to be a reb, sent a ball into the brush aiming by the sound. When that old musket went off there was a yell that waked the echoes for a mile around and he started a long line yelling. "Hol' on dar massa Linkum Sojer. I is a nigger,

I is. Doan shoot. Doan shoot. I done comin' in, I is. Whoop, hol' on dar 'delmity massa, hol' on, doan kill a po nigger dat done runned away from slabery." All this time the boys along the line were firing off their guns over his head into the hill. Finally he reached one of videttes, who commanded him to halt. Well he was a scared nigger if ever there was one, but he found freedom.

At another time one of the boys heard a thump, thump, thump coming down the hollow towards him and thought sure a Johnny was approaching. He lay quietly behind a stump until he could see the black object, was near enough to shoot when he sang out, "Halt, Halt or I fire," and the old cow lifted up her head said "baugh," then we had the laugh on the vidette.

We had strict orders not to allow anyone to pass the lines carrying anything contraband outside. Quinine, gun caps and late files of northern newspapers, especially.

There was a very bright and winsome country girl whose smile was sweet and winning, that frequently came into the lines, riding a bay horse. She always had a pass in and out, but in passing out was subject to a search for prohibited articles. One day she passed in when some of the regiment were on duty on the road over which she passed. When she approached on her return, she was stopped by the guard and politely requested to dismount. "Why," she said turning her beautiful eyes full on him while her little rosebud mouth put on its most fetching smile, "surely you would not ask a lady to dismount here and put her to so much inconvenience would you? You ought to be more gallant than that surely." "Well madam, we have our orders and must obey them," said he. So the dear little thing was lifted down which changed her sweet smiles to an ugly frown. Her sidesaddle was taken off and examined, quinine and gun caps were found stowed away in the seat, but no newspapers. After this was done the guard approached the now defiant girl and asked her if she had any newspapers and was answered in the negative. He then told her it became his duty to gently press her slender waist and heaving bosom to see that she did not have a copy somewhere about her beautiful form, and with blushes the poor fellow performed the delicate duty, finding quite a number of files of papers tucked in under her bodice next to her alabaster skin. How the poor trembling yank got them out will never appear in history unless she writes it. Relieved of the contraband goods she was assisted to mount and returned to Helena, but that sweet smile had vanished.

But with all our duties to draw our minds away from our condition the sadness of the situation could not be entirely eliminated from the thoughts or presence of the boys. Matters were discussed around the campfire, on the picket line in the silent watches of the night, and as we set by the side of our sick and dying comrades. And the conclusion reached by all was that no matter what happened we were there to stay until victory was ours or our bodies found resting places under a southern sun. Our daily prayer was that we might be sent into active service where we could help to achieve victories and bear the old flag forward.

E. E. Blake

It came April 11th, not a rumor but orders to go south. Never will I forget the cheers that went up when the order was read to regiment after regiment. Happy boys, they wanted war, active war and they got it.

On this date we were changed to the 2nd Brigade consisting of the 28th and the 24th Iowa, 56th Ohio and 47th Indiana, Col. Slack of the 47th commanding; in 12th Division, Gen. A. P. Hovey commanding; 13th Army Corps, Gen. John A. McClernand commanding. We boarded transports and proceeded to Milliken's Bend, Louisiana, where we landed and took up the march for Hard Times Landing sixty miles below, and below the Vicksburg batteries, where we became a part of the army under Grant. Our gunboats and a few transports having run by the batteries we took passage on them for Grand Gulf, a stronghold of the Confederates, at the mouth of the Big Black River, a bold bluff bristling with bayonets and terraced with cannon. It was Grant's intention to land troops and charge this stronghold under cover of the gunboats providing the rebel batteries could be silenced, but as they could not be, plans were changed and we took up the line of march past this stronghold. Our gunboats and transports running by them, we again embarked and landed on the Mississippi side of the river 15 miles below, drew three days rations and just at sundown started for Port Gibson, a distance of 20 miles. All night long with but occasional halts, we trudged along over the hills and through the deep ravines of that broken country.

THE 28TH IOWA INFANTRY

At about one o'clock a.m. we heard the muffled boom, boom, of a cannon in our front and again boom, boom. Our advance had found the rebels posted on a hill near Magnolia church, five miles from Port Gibson and exchanged a few shots from 10 pound guns, waking up the echoes that came reverberating over the hills to us as we advanced. Then the question: what was that? Did you hear that, boys? That was a cannon, or say, boys we have been "spileing" for a fight, we'll find it today, and so we did. We arrived at the foot of Thompson Hill at five a.m., tired and hungry. Gen. Hovey rode up and said "get a hasty breakfast boys, we must go into battle in a half hour. I want you fellows to remember your state today, and each man do his duty, be careful to obey every order of your commander quickly."

We got coffee boiled and had begun cooling and drinking it, when the artillery opened the ball and we were ordered into line and up the hill to our position. When we arrived at the crest of the hill we were ordered over a fence into a road to take position in line facing a rebel battery planted just across a ravine, then engaged in a duel with one of our batteries to the left of us. When the gunners saw us, they turned loose on us with grape and cannister, the road being depressed they did but little damage. We occupied this position for about an hour, when companies B, G and K were sent to assist the 34th Indiana in taking this battery. This was done by sending these companies to the left over a fence and hill in plain sight and but a short distance in front of the battery, then paying their respects to the boys on our right. When in position the charge was ordered, and down through a deep ravine through a black briar patch and up the hill into the battery we went with a cheer, and the guns together with 300 prisoners were ours, their line broken and forced back.

It was with a keen satisfaction we watched their broken lines as they went scurrying over the hills and away while we set up a cheer for the old flag and victory. We append here the report of Col. Connell from this point in the battle, who says:

> After this I reformed my command and was ordered to the extreme left (by Gen. McClernand) which was vigorously attacked by the enemy. Upon arriving at this point I found the enemy had massed a large force to turn our left flank, among which were two Missouri regiments, who were placed directly in our front. I formed my command so as to meet them and after a contest of nearly two hours the enemy fell back and we succeeded in planting the 8th Michigan battery on the knoll, we held against the enemy, which battery played with telling effect on their lines. At four o'clock they again appeared in force still attempting to turn our flank, but after a brisk engagement of an hour they retired in confusion.
>
> A company of skirmishers having been sent out to the left in front of our line discovered a rebel battery, which had command of the Port Gibson road.

THE 28TH IOWA INFANTRY

Our artillery soon got into position and commenced shelling them. My command lay in support until they had silenced the enemy's guns. By this time it was nearly dark, and Gen. Stephens coming up relieved us from the left, and we rejoined our brigade which was encamped for the night on the field. Here we lay on our arms in support of the Peoria battery during the night.

He further says:

With regard to the conduct of the officers and men during the action I can only speak in terms of highest praise. Although having marched all the day and night previous to the engagement carrying three day's rations and one hundred rounds of ammunition to the man, and having never been under fire before, they fought with that fearless spirit and determination, which has always characterized the American soldier.

Though hotly engaged from early morning until late at night, either in charging the rebel lines, repelling a charge, or supporting a battery, our casualties were few.

In the early morning we started on our way toward Port Gibson, four miles away, passing along the road over which the rebels had retreated, evidences of haste were strewn along the way such as guns, accoutrements, wagons, ambulances and many dead and wounded. Arriving at the beautiful little town of Port Gibson, we were glad to learn we were at rest for the day. A rest sorely needed by us after the experiences of the past few days. It was here the writer, then 20 years of age, first learned the enormity of the sin of slavery. While sitting on the steps to the balcony of one of the finest residences of the place, musing over the days just past, a beautiful girl of the brunette type dressed richly in striped silk, a prevailing style then worn by ladies in the South, came out and entered into conversation about the battle just over, the war and its causes, and in the course of our talk said "do you think we slaves will be freed?" "We slaves," said I, "are you a slave?" "Yes sir, I am a slave, I was bought by the master of the house for $3500, at New Orleans a few years ago. The master is now a colonel in the army." This beautiful girl, seven eighths white to one eighth Negro blood in her veins, then 20 years of age kept by a southern Col. as a slave to his besotted bestial lust; that alone caused me to see slavery in a light I had not thought possible and made me a "hated abolitionist" from that day until every shackle was stricken from every slave within our borders.

On the 3rd the forward move was begun and continued until we arrived at Big Sandy where we formed a line of battle on the 5th. On the 7th we moved up to Sand Ridge in front of the enemy. It must be remembered that but few of Grant's troops had crossed the river, that Johnson [Johnston] and Pemberton's combined forces more than doubled our strength, that we were in their country and had to develop their positions in every movement; therefore Grant was moving rapidly yet cautiously, and when he learned he had separated the two rebel armies, his plan of campaign was quickly made, and Sherman was dispatched with all the army but the 12th Division (Hovey's) to give Johnson [Johnston] battle, while our division was to make a demonstration against Pemberton who occupied a strong position at Edwards Depot. We began our advance on the 13th driving in his pickets and outposts. Had Pemberton known the facts no doubt we would have gotten tangled up with him before the day was done, but as he did not, we held him under the belief Grant's whole army was in his immediate front, until darkness came on, we then quietly filed away for Raymond, following in the rear of the balance of the troops.

Talk about rain. I have the impression there never was since the "original flood" such rains as fell during our march around from Edwards Depot, through Raymond, Clinton and back to Champion Hill. Mud and water waist deep, in which we were compelled to wade for hours on the march, mud for a bed and soft mud for a pillow, yet we slept and dreamed, awoke and renewed the march.

Passing through Raymond on the 14th, reached Clinton on the 15th, when an orderly brought good news that Jackson was captured and Johnson's [Johnston's] army driven across the Pearl River. No one not with us in that memorable campaign could ever appreciate what such cheering reports meant to us.

E. E. Blake

It meant success to our arms in the next battle, and Vicksburg's investment. It meant good hardtack and juicy sow belly to hungry stomachs now receiving but an occasional nubbin of green corn, or dry parched corn and a few green peaches as a daily allowance. One fellow describing his condition on this campaign said his eyes were sunken into his head so far, he could roll them down and see his own gizzard, and it was empty.

After remaining in Clinton a few hours we turned back on the Vicksburg road, reaching Bolton Station in the evening where we camped for the night, resuming our march May 16th. We encountered the rebel skirmishers two miles west of Bolton Station when company B were thrown out as skirmishers and the rebel line pushed back to the foot of Champion Hill, where we found Gen. Pemberton's army occupying an advantageous position on the crest of the hill, with a strong line at the base. It was eleven o'clock a. m. before we were formed for an advance, which was immediately made and in a short time the whole division was under fire and we began to realize we had hard fighting before us. In our advance we had to cross a ravine and ascend the hill through heavy timber and underbrush, driving the rebels' strong line of skirmishers before us, who behind trees, stumps and logs, would wait until our skirmishers approached, shoot them down at close range, then run for other cover further to the rear. The division closely following, our skirmishers soon pressed the Confederates to the crest of the hill, then it was the work of death began. The top of the hill was an open field behind which the rebs had

THE 28TH IOWA INFANTRY

formed strong lines and placed their batteries so to command all points. The nature of the ground was such we could not get our guns into position, therefore the battle on our part must be fought with small arms alone, until we could force them back and uncover the road and gallop a battery into action. Our advance continued under a murderous fire from the enemy and fighting became furious, every step reduced our force and men were falling by the score until at last we began to realize we in turn must fall back, and with a stubborn resistance we fought our way back, giving shot for shot until the gallant Crocker came to our support.

Then with a cheer and shout for victory we again moved steadily forward over ground twice fought over, now covered with the dead, wounded and dying of both armies. Oh, what a scene. No man can describe; comrades bleeding, dying, calling for help as you pass them by, but the battle was not won, the rebel lines lay just before us pouring in volley after volley into our advancing columns, their lines must be broken. The cheer of victory must resound over these smoke clad hills before our work was done. So with a charge and a yell the gallant Crocker's Brigade and our over-fought division pressed them back over the hill and down the slope across Baker's creek, their flight hastened by shells, dropped by batteries under Logan into their fleeing ranks, followed by Carr's, Logan's, Quimby's, and other divisions.

Hovey's Division having borne the brunt of this battle were ordered to remain on the field to bury the dead and care for the wounded. No pleasant task. I want to say as a matter of choice after three years active service and many battles, I would rather go into the battle with all dangers than be compelled to gather up the poor wounded groaning, bleeding, mangled bodies and carry them to the hospital for surgical treatment. And yet their condition and comradeship called out our human sympathies and our duties were faithfully performed. Then we laid ourselves down to rest under the spreading branches of the magnolia trees, but not to sleep. Thoughts of home and country, our dead messmates and sadly wounded comrades, filled our hearts with sorrow.

Blood, carnage, death, Oh the horrors of a field of battle, the roar of cannon, rattle of musketry, cheers of the charging columns, return yell of opposing forces, groans of the dying, pitiful cries of the wounded, all before your sight and in your hearing at the same time, makes up a picture that can never be described by brush or pen. Yet it was necessary to right the wrongs of a nation's sin in binding the shackles on four million human beings in this fair land.

General Hovey in his report of this action says "of the 24th and 28th Iowa in what language shall I speak. Not yet scarcely six months in the service and yet no troops ever showed more bravery or fought with more valor; of these and their commanders the state of Iowa may well be proud."

Grant in his memoirs says, "Hovey's Division bore the brunt of the battle. Lost in killed and wounded one-third of his division (1200), captured as many prisoners as he lost, and

THE 28TH IOWA INFANTRY

inflicted a heavy loss on the enemy in killed and wounded." We remained on the battle field until May 20th when we advanced to Black River and remained until the 24th guarding the bridge. The first night we lay here our lines ran along by an old log cabin then occupied by an old colored man and wife Dinah. On laying down for the night the regiment lay close alongside of Uncle Jake's cabin, who before retire to his couch of straw bowed him down before the Lord to pray and this is about what he offered up:

> O good Lawd, fadder ob de white mans and de po colled pusons, we done come befo de in prar. We done be po wicud sinful pusons we is, but dow am mussiful, dow is, and dow lubs dy chillin, bres de Lawd. Lawd wese happy dis nite we is, case de Linkum Sojer dey done come, yes de is, dey done layin on de groun by ole Jakes do dey is, Bres de Lawd. O Lawd, we is wufluss chillum, but wese bin prain fo mos a hunred yeas for de yea ob jubilee an you don foch it to us, bres de Lawd, Hallelija, bres de Lawd.

Just here one of the boys said Amen, and Uncle Jake broke out again.

> Yo hea dat Dinah, you hea dat, dem Sojers say Amen to Unc Jake, glory to de good Lawd dey is christens dey is, Hallelija. O Lawd dese Linkum Sojers dey done

get no pone, dey hungry dey is, dey mos starve, Lawd de done mind about chillin Isl, when in bondage to de gipicums when de sen de manna an de quail an dey coch em. Sen de hoe cake an de possum fat to dese Sojers an de chickns Lawd, let em roos low so dey kin coch em, case Lawd dey is come to foch de culled peoples outen slavery so dey no mo be whiped by de massa wif cat-o-none-tails, no mo go in de stocks. No mo be put in de shackles. Our chillen no mo be sole way down in Gorgey, po woman bar de chile no more be put in hole in grown, be whip. O Lawd, bres us all Amen, Amen, Hallelija Amen.

Such was the prayer of this old white headed slave, a simple prayer to the great God of nations, rude in construction 'tis true, but sublime in its simplicity and faith, who can say it did not reach the father's throne and bring an answer in his own good time.

On the 24th we left Black River and marched to our lines then being formed around Vicksburg, arriving at our position in the line on the 25th. Our camps were formed in the ravines back of Vicksburg and so close to the rebel works that minié balls and cannon shot and shell frequently came dropping over into our midst, often causing many ridiculous scenes. Our regiment was camped across a steep hollow, half on the steep hill on the north the other half on the south side. In order to get a level spot for tent and bunks, we would dig a notch in the hill then drive stakes in to support our bunks. One morning the Johns sent a conical shell over, which came tumbling down the hill knocking the stakes, demolishing tents and everything in its course; and being a shell and expected to explode every minute, caused some lively scampering among the boys for places of safety. Then some waggish fellow would stick his head out of his "Shebang" and yell, "Hunt yer hole Yank." Occasionally some luckless one got a spat from a minié ball and was taken away and buried out of sight or off to the hospital, so that all through the siege, we were constantly in danger of death or wound, either in camp or rifle pit, besides camped as we were, huddled in the deep ravines with water that was enough to kill the average man, the hot June sun pouring down its scorching rays until the very earth was smoking hot, it is no wonder many sickened and died and that our rudely constructed hospitals were constantly full. One day out of every four the regiment had to take its place in the pits going in at night and remaining until relieved the next night. We approached the rebel works by ditches zig zaging up the hills in such a manner as to be hid from the enemy's view until we got into our line of works. We usually carried one hundred rounds of ammunition for the day's shoot, expecting to kill as many Johnnies as it was possible to get a bead on and hit, but they very seldom showed their heads above works or their eye at port hole.

We often amused ourselves shooting down their "Bonnie blue flag" until they quit hanging them out, for it was a settled question that no treason's flag should wave in our presence for any length of time. The three days out of the advanced works were employed in guarding trains around to the Yazoo River, fifteen miles from our camp, loading supplies, and guarding back again, carrying ammunition up to our batteries, cleaning camps, cooking, chasing the ever present and always active grey backs and busy flea and occasionally indulging in a game of chuck-a-luck, mostly chucking against luck. Oftentimes of a still dark night we would climb to some high hill as close to the rebel works as possible and lay for hours watching the speeding shells from Porter's gun boat fleet above the city, as they described a circle in the air falling into the doomed city with a crash and roar that would shake the ground.

They were 200 pound shells filled with powder, bullets, scraps of iron and etc., with a long fuse that you could see blaze out as it wheeled up through the air until it would seem to stop, then begin to descend faster and faster, when, if the fuse was cut right it would explode above the city sending out its contents all over, hunting for some Johnny reb, sing, where are you Johnny, or Johnny hunt your hole for I am coming.

Sometimes they did not explode until they had buried themselves in the hard ground several feet. When this occurred there would be a small earthquake take place and a ton or two of dirt would be cast up. Once I remember a shell burst in a kennel of bloodhounds and started a yowl that only stopped when the dogs were dead or had got over their scare. Our rebel friends in order to escape these constant visitors dug caves in the hills and arranged living quarters therein where they were comparatively safe.

We very frequently held conversation with our gallant foes across the intervening space between lines. At other times would meet them between the lines and talk, swap coffee for tobacco and other articles, these meetings always occurring after the evening gun was fired, then war ceased for the night unless some demonstration was made by either side, then it was a fight. Once our pioneer corps was ordered to dig a line of pits close up to the rebel position, had a parley regarding it, finally pressed forward to begin the work and received a volley from a fort that sent them down the hill tumbling over one another. One of them, an Irishman, was asked why he did not fight the Johnnies and he replied, "to the divil wid ye. Do you be thinkin I could shoot wid me spade now?"

For some days prior to the 20th of June, great activity prevailed among the many batteries around the lines. Ammunition in larger quantities than usual was being carried up, and the boys began to speculate upon the possibilities of a charge on the rebel works, but early on the morning of the 20th we learned the cause. Grant had decided to show the boys on the other side what he could do by opening on them with every gun in position including Porter's gun boat fleet and mortar boats. I remember I had sat down in the pit and dozed off to sleep and was awakened from my dreams by the quivering earth beneath me and the vibrating air above and jumped up to see what had broken loose. A glance at the Confederate earthworks covered with splinters, flying dirt and smoke from bursting shells with not a Johnny in sight demonstrated clearly that in case we wanted to charge their works, our artillery could keep the enemy down until the charging columns were ready to scale the forts, making a sure success if it became necessary to make the attempt.

But this was not necessary for on the morning of the 4th of July according to the terms of surrender the boys in gray marched outside the works stacked arms and marched back again. We marched in and Vicksburg, the strong hold, was ours. How our hearts swelled with joy. With what satisfaction each number of the gallant 28th thought of the honorable part they had taken in the journey from Milliken's Bend west to the city around by Grand Gulf, Port Gibson, Big Sandy, Edwards Depot, Raymond, Clinton, Champions Hill, Black River, and the ever memorable siege, from May 1st to May 22d, marching, skirmishing, fighting day and night on but three days rations followed by 42 days siege, making more than two months of constant warfare hardly a moment out of hearing of the deadly shell or ping of minié ball, suffering with hunger and thirst, passing weary sleepless nights in mud and rain, yet ever in our places without a murmur. Vicksburg was ours, with its 31,609 prisoners, more than 200 cannons, all the small arms and stores besides, the great river was open from its source to the sea and we had helped to bring about this great end, but at a cost of many of our

THE 28TH IOWA INFANTRY

brave comrades who had gone down to rise no more forever, willing sacrifices for a beloved and bleeding country.

It would seem that after such continued and arduous service the army would be entitled to a little rest, but not so. The rebel General Johnson [Johnston] was at Jackson with a formidable army and Grant had determined to drive him out before resting, so an order came to be ready to move at 5 a.m. on July 5th. Rations were drawn, blankets rolled, a new supply of cartridges given out, the ranks dressed up , the old banner unfurled, and a little handful 250 in number, of the 956 that came out but eight months before, took up the march for Jackson back over the battle fields of May, with a shout and cheer.

On the advance on Vicksburg, a little old woman, once seen never to be forgotten and hard to describe, had warned us to look out for the Great Pemberton and his invincible Johnnies, assuring us Vicksburg could never be taken and on our return she came out from her cabin "do" with a smile on her wizened wrinkles face, a cob pipe between her lips and began, "Ah, ha, ah, ha, we'uns told you, we'uns did, we'uns told you'ns, you'ns couldent take Vicksburg. I knowed you'ns ed git liked, ye chicken theven yankee devils, git." So we left the old heifer to gloat for a day, then change her cob pipe to the other corner of her mouth and we pushed on toward Jackson.

It was amusing to see the aged patriarchs of the colored race as we passed by plantations on the route, (the aged alone were left, the young had run away to freedom), they would take off their old hat and say "fore God massa did you'ns take Vicksburg" and when told we had, it would be "Bres de Lawd. Massa dem Linkem Sojers jes fites like de debil dey does, bres the Lawd."

We reached Bolton Station on the 7th at 9 o'clock at night, camped or rather stopped, in an open field. It rained incessantly all night and in order to get a place to sleep the boys took rails from the fences laid across the ditches and laid their wet and tired bodies down thereon and slept. We were on the move at 5 a. m. of the 8th, continued the march all day and all night until 2 a. m. of the next day, when we lay down on our arms until morning, then were ordered forward to support Gen. Osterhouse, who had found the enemy. We halted eight miles from Jackson until the 10th when we were ordered to the left and took position. On the 11th, we began our advance and drove in the enemy's pickets and out posts forcing them back three miles, where we found them in force at three mile creek receiving their fire from a strip of woods across an open field back of the creek, here we threw out heavy pickets and remained through the night.

Beginning the advance in the morning, we drove the enemy back inside his works and began the erection of a line of breast works parallel with the enemy, here we remained until the night of the 17th, when a band came out on the Johnny fortifications and regaled us with the Bonnie blue flag and other southern airs, while Johnston and his army were silently putting the Pearl River between them and us, and Jackson, the hot bed of secession and treason, was ours for the second time. Much property was destroyed by our troops while here. Everything calculated to be of use in the Confederate service was fired. That rank rebel sheet, the *Mississippian* office, found a grave in its own ashes, a righteous judgement had over taken it.

On the 25th, we again took up the march for Vicksburg, arriving there on the 27th and went into camp on the bank of the river below the city. This trip to Jackson and return was one of the roughest of all the experiences we had had, because of the intense heat, frequent rains, muddy roads and constant movement, besides rations were scarce on the trip. Footsore and weary we were, many falling out by the way with sunstroke, while others fell sick and had to be left behind in the hospitals.

On the first of August we took boat for Natchez reaching there on the 3d. On the 4th we moved out to second creek, seven miles from Natchez and built a fort out of bales of cotton. Here it was thought we would remain for some time to rest and recuperate our failing health and strength, for we were beginning to grow thin and lank with such constant and trying ordeals as we just passed through.

It was while camped at this little fort we had a chance to learn something of the lives of the plantation slaves. While on picket on a by path in the woods some distance from camp, an old colored man, whose wool was white as snow, came along and I asked him if he could bring me something to eat and he said he would bring me some "conpone" and milk at midnight, if he and his old woman could get to me without being caught by the missus, who was a bitter rebel and on the watch for her slaves for fear they would leave her. Sure enough at about 12 o'clock they came, bringing the hoe cake, a small jug of milk, and a rooster whose squawk they had left on the plantation. While I sat and ate my pone and drank the milk they told me of their days of slavery for more than forty years on the same plantation, of the whipping post, the stocks, shackles, cat-o-nine tails, the brutality of the overseer, the frequent and awful whippings when the quivering flesh would be lacerated from head to feet of their naked bodies, then filled with salt to keep out the maggots. And then the old Auntie said, "Massa, I done don't forget dee poor woman dee bear de chile hab hole dug in gound and de lay in hole an be whip." The sin of a nation again. God required a sacrifice for sin and we were paying the penalty. Once paid there would be no more human slavery in this fair land, but at what a fearful cost to us and the generations to follow. Thanking the old couple for their generous supply of pone and milk and the old rooster brought me at their peril, I gave them a 50 cent scrip and they departed leaving me to spend the balance of the night on my lonely vigil.

We remained in this place but a few days, returning to Natchez. We again on the 12th embarked on board a transport and on the morning of the 13th awoke to see the light of New Orleans looming up in the distance. We landed at Carrollton above the city and went into camp in a beautiful plot of ground

THE 28TH IOWA INFANTRY

between Carrollton and the city. Here we received tents and cooking utensils. Fruit and vegetables were plenty and the boys began to live and grow. Our old and ragged clothes were cast aside, new ones put on and in a few weeks we began to feel like life was returning to us in earnest. Messes were formed, colored cooks hired and meals of fish, vegetables, macaroni, ice cream and fruit set up at but small cost to us, as the bacon, beans and rice drawn from our commissary found ready sale for cash at a high figure and the money spent by our cooks for something new and palatable, and everyday brought a healthful change in diet for us.

Our days were spent visiting the city and its environments, taking in the Shell Road, the Lake Pontchartrain, the battlefield of New Orleans, Henry Clay Monument, Jackson Park and the markets where many of the boys cultivated an acquaintance with beautiful dark eyed Creole ladies as they lingered over their custard pie, milk, fruit, and ice cream.

A whole month of rest, free from any service. Just one month of life then review by Generals Grant and Banks followed by an order to cross the river to Algiers and take cars for Brashear, ninety miles west down the coast towards Texas. This trip was made on flat cars first loaded with wagons and supplies, with troops, sandwiched in between, beneath and on top of everything, a wheezy old engine to haul us over a track that certainly had not been repaired since its building, having boards up every four miles marked, "go slow," four miles per hour, yet in the face of all this warning we were whirled over the line through swamps and bogs, lagoons, and over bayous through platoons of alligators lined up to watch us pass at the rate of 25 miles per hour. The motion of the cars cannot be described; it would make a dog sea sick.

But we "arrove," were ferried over the bay and went into camp to await developments. While waiting here for the rest of the troops designated for the expedition to come up, we spent the time hunting and fishing in the cypress swamps and bayous or arms of the bay. Raccoon, rabbits, and squirrels were plentiful, large black bass and other varieties of fish and sea crabs were easily taken, wild bees were found in dozens of trees about the camp. So the boys kept their time employed until Oct. 3rd, when we began a forward movement up the Bayou Teche through one of the most beautiful countries I ever saw. We moved by easy marches gathering fat beef, sweet potatoes, oranges, chickens turkeys and etc., at our leisure. Arriving at Opelonsas, one hundred miles from Brashear, on the 23d inst.

Strict orders against foraging were issued on the beginning of the march and obeyed about as it was expected by us when read to the boys on dress parade. One night after we got into camp, one of the boys came sneaking in with a good load of fat hens and was overtaken by the General, who said, "Here sir, what have you there?" "Chickens, sir," said the culprit, (soldiers never lied.) "You are under arrest, sir, orderly take him with all his fowls to my quarters," and up he went.

After a little time the General came, looked the hen thief over and asked "what regiment sir," was told.

"How many hens have you."

"Eight."

"Eight?"

"Yes, eight."

"How many in your mess?"

Answer, "four."

"All right there is four of us, you take four, leave me four, you can get more tomorrow, but mind don't get caught again. Now, go sir."

At another time one of the boys was in a patch of yams, prying out the great big yellow fellows, when the General came along and said, "what are you doing there?"

"Getting yams, sir."

"All right, don't dig more than you can carry," and rode on.

A great many of the people in this section were French or claimed to be and when we were marching through, claimed French protection by hanging out French flags. All good enough in their estimation, but a fat rooster or sheep from a plantation over which a flag of France floated, was just the same to us in those days as from one carrying the rebel colors.

Chaplain Simmons, in his history of the regiment, undertakes a description of these people, but fails to make it clear whether they are white or black, Negro, French or American. So I can only say they were all colors from a jet black to a pure white, with all the shades known to the human race sandwiched between, and as he says all shades in the same family. From my observation I should judge the mixing and blending of colors had been going on for the past century, until when a human being was turned out by the course of natural law, no matter what color its parents might be, no one could guess what color the offspring would be. Even after it had been seen it would not be safe to name the color for fear it would change when it got dry. However we are only writing of a certain class, the mixed breed.

This country contained many fine orange groves, sugar plantations with acres of brick buildings, that from a distance had the appearance of being a fair sized village. In fact when you take into account the large sugar houses, storage rooms, blacksmith shop, cooper shop, the residence of the planter, his barns and out buildings together with the negro quarters, where one or two thousand slaves lived, it went far to make up a very respectable village in size.

But to return to the regiment, on the 1st day of November we began to fall back. Although we had not had any trouble with the rebs in our advance or while laying in camp in Opelousas, as soon as we began a retrograde movement they began to follow us, hanging on our flanks and rear constantly, sending in a shot every chance they got.

We arrived at Carrion Crow Bayou on the 2nd, remained here until the 7th.

Gen. Burbridge's brigade being encamped at Grand Coteau, four miles in our rear, was attacked early on the morning of the 3d by a division of the enemy. The regiment with a part of the division were sent to his relief double quicking three miles. They went into the fight with the bayonet, meeting the Johnnies as they pressed Burbridge's command back in front and flank. When they met the cold steel of the new troops, they turned and fled leaving their dead and wounded to our tender mercy.

In this engagement the regiment did not get time to do much fighting, having met the rebel line with a bayonet charge that some way they never could or would stand. They broke and ran through the timber giving us only time enough for a few rounds before they were out of sight.

While we were engaged in fighting at Grand Coteau, the whelps attacked our camp we had just left, but the 24th Iowa reinforced by the sick, lame, and halt of the division, went to the assistance of the pickets and in a short sharp skirmish drove them away, killing two of them in the fight. The rebs having retreated, quiet was restored, and we returned to our camp.

On the 9th we fell back toward Vermillionville, being followed by the rebs. Once we formed to receive them, thinking we would have a brush, but they pulled off and we continued on our way camping at Vermillionville on the river, where we remained ten days fortifying the place. From here we fell back to New Iberia, and while there the weather grew extremely cold with a strong north wind blowing a gale. Being without tents and in light marching order it was something of a task to keep warm enough to sleep good, but old soldiers not being easily balked in any undertaking soon overcame the difficulty by rolling up in their blankets, then rolling into a dry ditch over which the wind swept, while we slept warm and comfortable undisturbed by the fierce gale. When on the picket line one day some of the boys found an opossum along a hedge and brought it to the post fire. Having heard the colored people tell of the sweetness "of de possum fat," they concluded they would have a great feast. So the 'possum was butchered and dressed up whole and carried to a French woman to be stuffed and baked for them, when done they all partook and in about an hour were all sick. Too much "possum fat" for the Yankee stomach.

Rebel sharpshooters were quite plenty about the lines and the orders were to keep a sentinel out some distance from the post, so to give warning of their approach, should they make a demonstration. On this day we sent out a typical Dutchman some 150 yards to the front (a new recruit he was) with careful instructions not to leave his place and to keep a sharp eye for Johnnies. "Yaw," he said, "I shust see the Johnnies I shoot and shust run fast as I can und told you vellers." We kept an eye on him for a while then busied ourselves about other matters and had about forgot Dutchie, when someone said, well were in blazes is that boy gone, I can't see him anywhere. A squad was formed and a search instituted. We looked all about the place where we had left him but no Shon. Finally one of the boys said, "I'll bet he has gone out to a house about a half mile distant near the timber," and thither we went. When nearing the house we heard a great commotion among the ducks and chickens under the house and stooping down we peered under and there was our boy trying to hook a straight stick around a duck's neck in order to draw it to him, and to the question, What are you doing John? he said, "Vy I ish dryin to get a dook or how many I can, tought ve ave dot vrench voman stop him mit rice, ve she macket dat possum." For fear of the approach of the Johnnies we hurried him out and back to the line, trying by the way to impress upon his mind the danger to him and the army in thus leaving his post. "Vell," he says, "I dank it bees all right, ve I got von dook."

Having gathered all the sugar in the country, we broke camp on the 19th of December and marching 25 miles each day, reached Berwick on the 21st, foot sore and weary. It was the last day of this 50 mile pull, one fellow offered to bet a dollar greenback he had a blister on his foot as big as the bill, which bet was taken and he won, for the whole bottom of his foot was a blister, yet he travelled 25 miles that day. Who can tell of his sufferings. One fellow after reaching camp and throwing himself down on the ground broke out with "Ye ma talk ave the fire eaters, ave the South and the copperheads ave the North, but be me sawl for sedden dath gime a knapsack."

We crossed Berwick Bay on the 23rd and on Christmas day took cars for Algiers, where we arrived late in the night and went into camp. If any man, in or out of the army can tell why this expedition was sent out I would like to hear it. It seemed then (and does to this day) as if the man that planned it did not know what he was doing. It seemed to have no definite object and nothing was accomplished except a wearing out of those who made the trip.

We remained in Algiers three miserable weeks, camped part of the time in the open, the weather was cold, it rained incessantly, so our camp became one sea of mud outside our tents. We used to take a board and scrape it up into pools then lay cord wood to keep it from spreading out again, thus keeping a pathway between quarters, so we could get in or out our tents. One night about 10 o'clock one of the boys, who was in the habit of taking on more whiskey than he could carry, came into camp swearing at the mud, struck his toes against a stick of wood and pitched forward into a pile of mud six inches deep, and when he landed his mouth was open, and mouth, eyes and nose were completely filled. Had we not heard him and gave him assistance he would have died, as it was, we had trouble to get the mud out and the wind into the fellow. One thing it did, it scared him sober so he was able to get out of his garments of filth.

The camp became so muddy, cold and frozen with ice, we were compelled to abandon it and were moved into the large Belle View Iron Works, where we were free from mud, but as all our campfires were built inside and no way for the smoke to escape, we were forced to weep over the situation. Red eyes was the order of the day and no one escaped the blinding smoke day or night, so that our condition so far as comfort was concerned, was but very little improved. We frequently went over into New Orleans for a day's outing, often remaining for the theater, getting back on the midnight boat, thus escaping all we could of camp life. A few days later, about the 19th, we crossed over, marched through the city, got aboard the cars and were set down at Lake Port, where we boarded the beautiful new Gulf Steamer *Gen. Banks* and were carried over Lake Pontchartrain to Madisonville, some two miles up the Pearl River, a small village in the piney woods. Here we fixed up quarters and began the building of fortifications. We then thought we would advance on Mobile as an objective point, while here we received quite a number of recruits.

Many of our sick returned to us and the health of the regiment had improved so, we could muster quite a line of hardy looking men quite in contrast to our appearance after the Vicksburg campaign was over. We remained at this place about a month working on the forts, doing picket duty, attending church and cultivating the acquaintance of the French lasses of the town.

It was here, occurred one of the most laughable incidents connected with our service. A squad of Co. G were on post on the road running out east on the sand ridge. We supposed we were the last post on the north end of the line of pickets, but not so, one of the New York regiments had a line running down along the swamp, through heavy underbrush and had cut a path up to the road, a few yards east of our post. On this beat was a great big overgrown Irishman with wool in his teeth and the map of the old sod on his face. Just after daylight as we sat on a log talking, this Pat came strolling up this path towards the road, with his loaded musket cocked upon his shoulder. When near the road he stubbed his toe and fell his full length forward pitching his gun ahead of him, the hammer striking a stub, a minié ball and streak of fire shot across the road in our front.

We bounded up, grabbed our guns and prepared for a fight when one of the boys saw the fellow and said, "sit down boys, its only and Irishman ordering arms." By this time he had begun to get up and this is what he said. "To hill wid America, do yez moind that noo. When I left the ould sod begorra did the na soi Amirica was a free country? Whin oi landed in Noo Yourk bejabers, who shod mate me but a divil of a mon, and he said to me, says he, oui am glad yer coom Pat, coom and toik a dhrink and mate the bys, an I wint of coorse as a gintleman wod, an by the saints above me whin I waked up in the marnin I war a soger too, sorra the day, an here oi am fallin doon over the sticks and stubs skinning me laigs and brusin me bones an shootin off me ould gun in the bushes beyant. To hill wid America, begorra ol wish ol was in ould Dublin noo." And he turned and vanished down the path leaving us convulsed with laughter, not so much at his words, as the manner in which he said them.

The days spent at this quiet spot, comparatively free from danger, were days we always remembered as our best during our service, but they could not last, and Feb. 26th we were ordered back to New Orleans to prepare for that ever memorable

THE 28TH IOWA INFANTRY

campaign up Red River under Banks. We arrived in Algiers on March 1st and went into camp remaining until the 4th. When our experience of a few months before was repeated by a ninety mile ride over the same old road to Brashier on Berwick Bay, most of this ride was made in the night that was as dark as night could possibly be, on the way one of the boxes on the truck got hot and the packing took fire, blazing out its flashes of light from under the car. Many of the boys not knowing much about cars got the impression the axle would burn off and let them down and they set up a yell to stop the train yelling at the top of their voices, "cars a fire pass the word forward to the engineer to stop," but there was no stop, on and on we flew while brighter grew the flame until others became panic stricken and took up the yell making the welkin ring with their shouts, causing the owls to take up the cry and the alligators to lift their tails in wonder. Finally a water tank was reached and the fire extinguished. Arriving at Brashear we were ferried over the bay, our camp and garrison equipage turned over, every one reduced to light marching order, the sick and lame and all those not capable of long hard marching left behind and returned to New Orleans; and Sunday morning our regiment 550 strong pulled out over the old Bayou Teche route preceded by the cavalry and the 19th A. C. It was understood that Shreveport, on the Red River, was our destination, and we marked it down as a fight from start to finish as it afterwards proved.

On the 17th we moved forward, passed Franklin and New

E. E. Blake

Iberia camping one night at camp Pratt, skirmishing in front had begun; next day we approached Grand Coteau, where we had the fight some months before, here Confederates threatened our trains and caused us a four mile double quick march. The day following we passed through Opelousas and Washington, camping at Bayou Bouef, laying here one day. We then pushed forward and five days afterwards landed in Alexandria a distance of one hundred miles. Those who have read *Uncle Tom's Cabin* will remember Cheneyville and Bayou Bouef and the Lagree plantation, the home of Uncle Tom, a cabin on this plantation was pointed out as the original Uncle Tom's cabin. This country was rich in corn, sugarcane and cotton, some of the richest plantations in all the southland were found here along this Bayou. No Yankees having entered this territory before, gave us a glimpse of slavery as it had existed for a century, it was here a long haired planter came to our regiment and offered a hundred dollars for his negro, that had taken up the march for freedom. He was given one minute to clear the lines and he stood not upon the order of his going but skipped out.

It was a sight to behold the colored people on these plantations as we approached each in succession, no matter what they were doing as soon as the old drum began to beat they would throw down the hoe and come trooping across the field to see the Yankee sojer, shouting and singing. Long before we would reach the negro quarters the fences would be lined with black-faced, wooly-headed pickannies that looked like

THE 28TH IOWA INFANTRY

a row of buzzards at a roast. These people had been told all manner of stories about the Yankee soldiers, that they were devils, had horns, long tails and cloven feet and would kill all niggars they got a hold of, but these stories were not believed and though they were uneducated and ignorant, yet some way they understood all about the war and what it meant to them and hailed with joy unspeakable our approach, they went wild with joy, one old auntie climbed upon the fence spread out her hands toward heaven and shouted, "Oh my! Oh my! I is so happy de Linkum sogers done come, dey is, an dey aint got horns eider, bress de Lawd." We quote from Chaplain Simmons history here.

> "Where are the rebs aunty?" said we, to an old woman standing on top of the fence, "Oh dey flew like the birds and I does pray de Lawd dat you may sweep dem from de earf," and her voice was lost in the passing column. Two old ladies on the opposite side of the bayou were jumping for joy in the wildest frenzy; one of them looked more like a huge pile of liver, with a blanket thrown over it, than a human being, in the top of which rolled a pair of enormous eyes underset by a well-developed row of ivory, ranging round a mouth that reminded you of an open carpet bag hung up by the handle, and still possessed somewhat the appearance of a semi-human form. The other, a neater specimen of negro, dressed in rags of dirt color,

but with features lighted up with joy, as though a thousand Italian sunbeams had concentrated in her heart bursting out through every pore of her soul in a flood of gladness. Each seemed to be assisting the other in keeping time to the music of their own hearts. We thought of glad women, proud women, happy women; but these were more than all of them. The martial music of the bands stirred them into wilder revelry. We thought of the year of jubilee and they seemed fully to appreciate the idea "Old massa run away" and as for the overseer—

"We locked him up in de smoke-house cellar,
And de key trown in de well."

Some shouted, some prayed, while others danced to the music of their jubilant hearts; who could blame them, freedom was at hand.

We reached Alexandria Saturday and for a wonder rested on the Sabbath day.

Everybody in the regiment recognized the ability of the boys of Co. B. to smell out everything dead or alive no matter where located, but when the news was brought to camp that they had dug up three barrels of whiskey in a grave yard it created no little surprise until we learned who it was that traced the find. Some fellows could smell whiskey further than a buzzard would a carrion, therefore the Johnnies made a mistake when they buried the whiskey but they were not

THE 28TH IOWA INFANTRY

acquainted with Co. B. at that time. The finding of the booze created no small amount of merriment in camp and a very hilarious condition to the boys who drank it, which was not confined to "B," for with all their faults there were a generous lot and would divide on occasions like this.

On Monday morning, the 28th, we took the lead, we were in close proximity to the Johnnies and as was, or had been the case, we were first in and last out of all scrimmages. Gen. [Albert L.] Lee's cavalry were in advance of us and it was expected we would be in support of him whenever he found the rebs too strong for his force. It was 85 miles to Natchez, this distance we covered in three days and a half making the last 25 miles in less than six hours, finding the rebs in strong force contesting the advance of our cavalry. Reaching the city we formed a line across the town, stacked arms, and began to look about us for something to eat. The Catholic people had a school and nunnery here presided over by a Mother Superior and a corps of teachers; it was a large building with a basement in which the people had gathered their sheep, pigs, turkeys, chickens and ducks for safe keeping, thinking, no divil of a yank would dare to enter for the purpose of plunder. When the boys found the fowls of the air and four-footed beasts all penned up they said "here's a rum go," and proceeded to open up the doors. The good mother came to protest saying surely you will respect the sacredness of the institution and not desecrate so holy a place by entering to steal, surely you respect the things belonging to God and his holy church. To which respectful speech one of the boys replied that he had read in the Bible somewhere that a sheet had been let down from heaven in the presence of St. Peter, filled with all manner of beasts of the earth and the fowls of the air, and Peter had been told to arise and eat, by the angel of the Lord, and if the Lord was so anxious for Peter to have a full belly he had no doubt He would approve of us, his servants, helping ourselves to what the Holy church of St. Peter had penned up. That the boys were not used to ladies society and if they did not want their feathers ruffled they had better retire to the upper chambers, where they would be perfectly safe and could watch the boys doing the skinning act. They gracefully retired, and wool, hair and feathers began to move lively. Now we accepted this as a part of the goodness of the Lord to us through the agency of the good mother church, for we were tired and foot-sore and not very well able to run after our meat; we got it just the same. We remained here some days, were reviewed by Gen. Banks who complimented us on our ability to march and never mentioned our foraging qualities.

Natchitioches (Nacitosh) is situated about five miles from Grand Ecore, on the Red River. It was the rendezvous of the 3rd and 4th U. S. Infantry just preceding the Mexican War, and was Gen. Grant's stopping place before leaving for the seat of war at its outbreak. While we rested here Lee's cavalrymen were constantly skirmishing with the enemy, finding them in strong bodies at different points in our front, which fact was reported daily to Gen. Banks, a fact that has always seemed to me sufficient to warn any man in command of such an expedition to move with caution and prudence, especially as we were so near the place we had started out to capture and destroy, and knew we must fight at least one hard battle before our success was assured. But from his actions then and the two days to follow, his utter inability to comprehend the situation or meet the requirements of fair generalship proved to every private in the command that the government had made a mistake and spoiled a good statesman to make a very poor general.

On the 6th we took up the march, marched all day and night, in the morning received orders to hurry up to the support of Lee, and hurried forward to Pleasant Hill. Here we laid down to await developments. Shortly afterwards the cavalry found them again and called for us, we responded double quicking out two miles to their support, when the Confederates fell back again and we returned to Pleasant Hill. We were now the 3d Division of the 13th Corps. Again the enemy had checked the cavalry, and the 4th Division of the 13th Corps took the lead in their support, our little corps following them. The cavalry having found the Johnnies in force at Ten Mile creek on the morning of the 8th, we were hurried forward reaching there about noon. Here we halted to await further developments. All the time we lay here Bank's cavalry train of wagons and ambulances were pushing to the front along a road that was worn into the hills so deep they could not turn out, or be turned around. In place of parking his trains and hurrying forward the troops, he pushed the cavalry and two small divisions, say 4,000 men, to the front, then filled up the only road over which troops could approach the battle-field with wagons and ambulances, then ordered the cavalry to attack the enemy which they did, being repulsed. Gen. Lee sent an orderly with a dispatch to Banks (then with us) that the enemy were in force and strongly posted and he could not dislodge them, then the 4th div. 13th A. C. were put in to help break through 28,000 rebels. They with the cavalry gallantly charged and were cut to pieces. Then came an order for reinforcements and the 3d div. 13th A. C., about three thousand, were double quicked four miles, swinging into the line by a flank movement.

Loading our guns on the run we met the cavalry and 4th div. coming out in fragments and the victorious rebs marching on, we pushed forward through their shattered lines and with one of our old time yells of defiance, opened out on their advancing columns and checked their advance. The enemy began pouring in shot and shell, we fighting fast and furious to hold our position hoping for help from the 19th Corps, 3,000 against 28,000 at close range. It was a death struggle. We had never been defeated and we counted every shot for victory. For two hours we held them, then our ammunition gave out, the last ball was fired, the enemy was pouring around our flank closing in on our rear, when Gen. Franklin road quickly along the lines and said, "boys, you have done all you can, save yourselves if you can," and we started to the rear

THE 28TH IOWA INFANTRY

leaving our Colonel and eighty-seven brave boys on the field. We had not moved very far back of our line in battle until the rebel cavalry were crossing at right angles commanding us to surrender which many of us did. I want to say right here, it is not a very safe or pleasant place to be in, when you have to stand before a half dozen cocked carbines in the hands of drunken rebels, with muzzles pointed straight at you and not four feet distant. Such was the sad experience of many of us before we got off this field of carnage.

We were ordered to pass back into the rebel lines by our captors, while they went for Bank's cracker wagons and began filling up their haversacks, and we, well we made a run for liberty and won. No man can picture such a scene as was enacted on that bloody field on the 8th day of April 1864. Picture to yourself a field covered with dead and wounded of both armies, Yanks a foot, on horseback and on mules, rebel infantry, and cavalry, teamsters, negroes, wenches, artillery horses, and mule teams, ambulance teams and drivers, all in a mad rush, our part of it for the rear, and the Johnnies for the cracker wagons, with yells, curses, groans, neigh of horses, rattling chains, bray of mules, roar of cannon and rattle of musketry, then tell me what you would liken it to. One of the boys who got up just in time to meet the swirl as it came rushing through the pine woods said it sounded to him like all hell had broke loose and there was no way to stop it, and I have often thought he was about right.

Our Chaplain, who was always at the front when a battle

was on, was caught in the mad rush to the rear and was mounted on Major Myers' mare, which did not seem to get over the ground as fast as he wanted her to, and when seen by some of the boys was urging her forward with all of his might. Leaning forward in his saddle he seemed to be pushing on the reins to help her along; when joked about it afterwards by one of the boys he said, "Well Israel, the fact of it is, I never felt so far from my mother in all my life before as I did coming out of that scrape and I was bending all my energies and that of the mare to reach a safe place."

Think of it, all this happening to a little band of 4,000 infantry and a handful of jaded, worn out cavalry in the broad sunlight, with 16,000 good men but eight miles away, and A. J. Smith's 10,000 Western boys at Pleasant Hill but fifteen miles away, with no reason under heaven why they could not have been up to our support, then it would have been an easy victory instead of a disgraceful defeat. It makes one's blood boil to this day to think of it.

But two miles back we met the 19th Corps, and night coming on, the rebels stopped the pursuit and the army fell back to Pleasant Hill and began preparations for another bout with the now victorious foe. The lines were formed and the trains (what the rebs had not captured) were sent to the rear toward Grand Ecore, accompanied by the 3d and 4th Divisions of the 13th Corps, now reduced to but a handful, as guards. We were now in for another day's march, and had not slept for thirty-six hours. In the meantime the roar of

THE 28TH IOWA INFANTRY

cannon and rattle of musketry around Pleasant Hill gave notice of hard fighting, the Johnnies flushed with victory, came on pouring out of the timber into the open field to be met by Smith's brave boys, and the 19th Corps with masked batteries, and what they had counted on as sure victory proved to be a repulse of their whole command with great slaughter and a recapture of our train and batteries lost the day before. And had Banks turned his whole army about and followed up this victory the result to the rebels would have proved doubly disastrous. Shreveport would have been captured and the expedition a success; but no, a retreat in the face of victory was ordered and all night long tired, sleepy and hungry we plodded along sleeping as we marched. The night was intensely dark, and in order to light the way fires were built with pine knots lighting the dark recesses of the forest causing a grand and weird appearance to the scenery about us. Rebel cavalry were skirting our flanks keeping us ever on the lookout for a charge, thus one of the darkest and saddest nights in the regiment history was passed.

At 2 o'clock that day we went into camp fifteen miles from Grand Ecore, the next morning we continued the march to the river taking position on the Natchitoches Road in front of Grand Ecore and began the erection of defensive works, expecting an attack of the enemy, who it was reported were advancing in force having been reinforced by Price from Arkansas. Here we had time for a review of the past four days and a thought for the gallant Colonel and more than eighty comrades left on the field of battle. We had marched fifty-five miles, fought one hard battle and many smaller ones in the past forty-eight hours without a moment to sleep or an hour to prepare coffee or a warm meal. Our hard tack was full of worms and had to be eaten in the darkness where they could not be seen. Our comrades lay dead or wounded on the field of battle, we knew not their fate. Our eyes were heavy for want of sleep, our bodies weary for want of rest, our stomachs empty for want of palatable grub to eat, and our hearts sad because of the fate of our comrades. Our indignation and utter contempt for those who were responsible for a condition of affairs that common prudence could have averted was beyond expression, our condition was deplorably sad. It was one of the misfortunes of war and we accepted it with as good grace as possible and prepared for duties yet to devolve upon us.

Our transports had passed up the river and had got into some trouble which necessitated a delay of some ten days in our movements. The rebels being advised of our intended retreat marched by us here and took position on our front ready to oppose our advance down the river. On the 23d our transports and gunboats having returned we got in line at 5 p. m. ready to move, but owing to some hitch in the movements of our trains we did not get started until daylight next morning. We marched all day and night halting at 2 o'clock a. m. for a couple of hours, then moved forward again until we approached Cane River. Here we found the festive rebel

THE 28TH IOWA INFANTRY

Gen. Bee had preceded us and had planted batteries on the high hills commanding the approach to the bridge and had thrown up breast-works and intrenched his command in a strong position, disputing our passage over the bridge, thus checking our advance, while Dick Taylor pressed Smith on our rear, thus placing us between two fires.

Trains were halted and the brigade left to hold our side of the river, batteries planted to shell the rebel line, and we quietly waded the river waist deep above the Confederates and made a sneak to the rear and before Bee had time to realize what had happened. We were mercilessly plugging them in the rear. It was a short sharp and bloody encounter resulting in a defeat to the busy Bee and his division, and a heavy loss in men and guns. Had we been familiar with the lay of the ground, we would have captured his whole force, as it was they got out by the skin of their teeth. While we were thus engaged Gen. A. J. Smith and his two divisions were hotly engaged, with Dick Taylor gaining a decided advantage repulsing him with considerable loss. Here we prepared for a night's rest, but were soon called out in support of the cavalry, who had overtaken the retreating rebs. By the time we arrived the fight was over, and we returned, built up fires and dried our wet clothes, made coffee, cooked pig and made a comfortable night of it after the hardships of the days past.

In the early morning we were awakened by the cannon's sullen roar in our rear, where Smith and Taylor were having a breakfast spell.

E. E. Blake

From this point begins the negro exodus. They were watching for our return, and had all their scanty belongings ready packed, and when the columns began to move the darker column began to augment. They came from all directions at all times of the day and night, all sizes, ages and conditions, from the old man whose hair was white as wool to the child born the day before, from the little bead eyed kid to the old aunty, whose size and weight would seem to bar the possibility of her ever keeping pace with the army. Here you would see a family of eight, the husband with a bundle on his back topped out with a kinky headed boy, the wife with her bundle and a child at breast leading another, while trudging along by her side were the balance, each carrying some article. One old man so weak from old age he could scarcely get up when down, was found in the ranks. When asked how old he was, he said, "For God Massa mos two hunred I guess." Well where are you going? "Ise goin wid you'ns all massa, I wants to die a free man, de good Lawd he took car of me, he will." And while our columns kept the road, two lines of dusky travelers four deep kept pace with us on either side, hundreds, thousands, fleeing from slavery's chain, poor, ignorant, homeless creatures. How we pitied them, none could blame, who boasted such a thing as a heart within his anatomy.

Our sufferings were great as we toiled over the hills and vales of this south land, we often thought, these poor wretches suffered ten fold more than we in the weary days

THE 28TH IOWA INFANTRY

and nights that followed, before they reached a place where the government could care for them.

From the battle field at cane River, we took a road that lead through a pine forest for twelve miles, then merged out of the timber to Kappidise Bayou and Red River. Here we halted at midnight and lay down to rest without supper. Resuming the march in the morning we reached Alexandria, and that day went into camp. We now felt we were well on our way back towards New Orleans and our mail from home.

Here we were met by the paymaster and paid that munificent sum there has always been so much kicking about, 16 dollars a month, for which we went out to battle. Well, we were glad to get it and were not long in spending it for such things as we sorely stood in need of.

But our rest was short. On April 30th the regiment was thrown out two miles as guards, and were not long in kicking up a fight, which at one time threatened to become general and engage the whole army. On the next day we were ordered out with two days rations, other troops following. After an advance of about two miles we stirred up the Confederates again, having a lively bout with them, fell back to avoid bringing on a general fight, the Confederates following us up.

Early the following morning while our coffee was boiling on our rail fires, the impudent whelps opened on us with a battery of six pound guns, scattering our fires, spilling our coffee and filling our eyes with dirt. The atmosphere took on something of a sulphurous hue about this time.

E. E. Blake

There were a few, not loud but deep, cuss words strung out in sections, guns were shouldered and the fun began. The 28th Regiment were thrown in front and the advance began. We moved steadily forward, followed by other troops, engaging the enemy in a very heavy skirmish early in the morning. In order to give some understanding of the nature and extent of this continuous battle, I want to say that the country over which it was fought was a level bottom between the Red River and a bayou and the swamp on the South, which was heavily timbered. The bottom was crossed by strips of timber, occasionally a narrow bayou, and open fields enclosed by rose hedges.

The enemy would plant his batteries behind one of those bayous or in a strip of timber and await our approach and as we advanced pour into the ranks shot and shell. Yet the line would move steadily on until we came in close range, then we would go for them with the bayonet, they would limber up their guns and fall back in quick time to another bayou or strip of timber and begin the same tactics. To show something of the excitement attending these advances, I will tell of some things that happened which came under personal observation. We had advanced into an open field and had halted when the rebs sent a 6 pound ball through the ranks of Company B, passing between two of the boys catching the haversack of one and cartridge box of another, sent them whirling round and round and deposited them across a corn row, sick from the exercise. About this time a big German in Company G was hit by a minié ball in the heel of his big flat shoe and his feet were carried from under him with such force it nearly broke him in two, how he swore at the "domed younies." Our Colonel riding along on his spirited buckskin horse had a shell burst directly under him causing the horse to leap up into the air like he had wings. One of our generals thought to stop awhile by the side of a cabin with a chimney built of sticks and mortar, when a ball from a battery took off the top four rows of sticks, dropping them over his head like a collar.

Four skirmishers thought to shield themselves behind a dry log laying parallel with our lines when a solid shot struck it, bounding it up until the boys could see through under it. These with a hundred other exciting incidents went to make up the day's battle under peculiar circumstances. The regiment started out mad, and everything tended to increase their madness. After coolly marching up within fighting distance through shot and shell, and when just ready to begin our work to have them run like cowards was too much for the boys, and they would indulge in some very profane talk and give the rebs a few volleys as they ran. Along in the afternoon the Confederates fell back behind a bayou about 20 yards wide and ten feet deep, in the bottom of which there was perhaps a foot of water and four feet of mud, they then took rails and made crossings every 20 or 30 feet, and crossing over advanced to a hedge towards which we were marching and began whacking away at our advancing columns, thinking when we got too close they would fall back and cross on their rails, mount their horses and retreat as before. But it did not work so well this time; the old 3d Division had its blood up and were moving rapidly forward, and at the first rush of smoke from that hedge made a rush for the rebs they were not anticipating. They broke over the hedge and gave chase, gaining every jump on the now thoroughly scared Johnnies, pressing them so close their artillery could not fire on us without first hitting their own men and becoming alarmed at our near approach limbered up and flew to the rear, followed by shells from the batteries.

We pressed these fleeing rebs so close that they did not have time to cross on the rails and would sail off the bank into the mud, then scramble for the dry land. Our fellows followed so close some of them crossed over and pulled the rebs off their horses before they got fairly into the saddle. We fired at and yelled after those that got away as long as we could see a bunch of long hair flying in the wind. After the chase we advanced some distance further up the valley, but the Confederates had crossed the swamp and taken to the woods. Here our pickets shot and killed a rebel major, one of Gen. Bee's aids de camp who was creeping onto the line with the purpose of shooting a yank.

This ended the day's excitement and we returned to middle Bayou, having fought all day driving the rebs fifteen miles, chasing and charging them from early morn to late in the day. Gen. Green in speaking of the regiment's action in this day's work, said, its fortitude and coolness called out the praises of

THE 28TH IOWA INFANTRY

the whole division. We were fighting and skirmishing all the time we were here, which was nearly two weeks.

When our gunboats and transports passed up the Red River, it was an easy matter for them to pass over the rapids near Alexandria, but on their return it was found the river had fallen so the gunboats could not pass, and it became necessary to build a dam on either side out into the stream so as to increase the stage of water in the channel between to a sufficient depth to float them over the rapids. It took about two weeks to accomplish this and when done and the gunboats safely passed, we, on the 13th of May, began our march toward Atchafalaya.

Our corps marched in line by the side of the trains, the 19th Corps in front while A. J. Smith's Division brought up the rear. The enemy were hanging on our flanks day and night, occasionally pitching into Smith's rear guard causing him to have to stop and fight. When near Mansura, or Darkville, the enemy formed in our front and planted batteries opposing the advance. Our trains were lined up, lines formed for battle and an advance began. The Confederates had formed a line across a prairie eight miles square with their batteries lined across behind their troops; back of these were their trains. We began driving them back on the west side, advancing our batteries in the same order, infantry following and trains in a parallel line so in advancing we could have a full view of the whole Confederate army as they fell back and our lines as they advanced.

E. E. Blake

It was an imposing sight. We pressed them back across this field keeping up a steady cannonade. We advancing and they fighting and falling back until the enemy reached the woods, when they drew off on a road leading back around to our rear leaving us to pursue our way. On reaching Atchafalaya, Gen. Smith bringing up the rear had a spirited engagement whereby the Confederates lost some two hundred men, which ended the troubles of the memorable Red River Expedition under Banks that will go down in history as one made up a series of mistakes and blunders on the part of the one in command that were almost criminal. The record made by the 28th was one the regiment as well as the state from which it came may well be proud. Every man was in his place. Every service required of them was faithfully performed.

Whenever there was a fight they were in it. If it was a charge to be made they never faltered. They went out to fight.

From Atchafalaya Bayou we marched to Morganzie Bend on the banks of the Mississippi and went into camp. Here we were met by numerous sutlers with large invoices of goods, groceries, bottled liquor and canned stuff of all descriptions. These sharks had been robbing the boys in times past to such an extent that they did not hold them in high esteem, so they began to plan for a charge.

The word was passed around at 7 o'clock p. m.: a rush was to be made and the shops looted. At sharp 7 o'clock the fun began and in less than five minutes, we had taken the canvas fort and all its contents, most of which was going into a corn

THE 28TH IOWA INFANTRY

field in the rear of the camp. Sutlers did not bother us any more. It was some days before we had eaten and drank all the good things these hooked nosed gentlemen brought us. They left us wiser than they came, and with a lighter purse than they had intended.

Occasionally some enterprising skunk would play a joke on the boys that caused us no end of fun. One day one of the boys found a case of canned beef up the river some distance, he opened a box and found it spoiled, he could not eat it, but knowing the boys' love for canned goods, concluded he could sell every can if he worked it right, so he got two logs and some boards together, built him a raft, loaded on his case of beef and put out into the river, sailing his craft up to the bank near the regiment, he yelled out, "canned beef 50 cents per can" and the boys bit, buying every can before anyone thought to examine it, then he laughed and walked off with his shin plasters leaving the boys who purchased spoiled beef to howl.

One morning right early as a squad of us were laying on top of the Levee on picket, where the road made a sharp turn around an angle, we heard some one out in front shouting like a backwoods preacher at a camp meeting and wondered what in the world it could mean. We lay and watched and listened, soon we saw a young cavalry lieutenant of a New York regiment emerging from the woods, the reins of his bridle thrown down on his chargers neck, his head thrown back and his arms pawing the air. We wondered if the fellow was crazy. He was not, he was making a speech all by himself, soon he came close enough for us to hear and this is what he said, "You may call me a democrat, you may call me a Copperhead, or you may call me a republican or what not, it makes no difference to me what you call me, one thing is damn sure I stand for the Union" and we all said, "bully for you old man." Well, if you could have seen that fellow grab his bridle, spur his horse and get, you would have laughed as we did, we scared the speech all out of him and I warrant when he got home on his furlough and was called on for his speech, he could not think of a word of it, and the girl he left behind never knew what an orator he had been.

We remained here at Morganzie Bend until the 13th of June, when we embarked on board boats for New Orleans again, arriving there buoyant and hopeful.

A few days thereafter Col. Connell, who had lost an arm and was made prisoner the 8th of April at Sabine Cross Roads, returned to the regiment bringing the first news we had had of our boys left on that fated field.

On the 20th we marched up the river to the little town of Kennerville, where we felt assured we would be permitted to rest for some time and recuperate, but not so. Dick Taylor was reported as moving on Brashier. A boat was sent up and we were taken to Algiers again, and again boarded the same old flat cars and were set down at Thibadeauxville, June 28th. Here we gave the people of this benighted land an old fashioned Fourth of July celebration, something new to them. One old fellow said he had lived there fourteen years and had never seen a celebration before.

While here we were regaled with water melons as large as a bushel basket, brought in by the colored men by boat loads on the bayou that ran past the town. Water melons grow to perfection in this climate, so did the festive gallinipper and bellowing alligators. This country also produced some very rank and saucy secessionists of the female gender, whose tongues were as long and as sharp as some that grew north of Mason and Dixon's line. This we had occasion to find out in our perambulations about that Frenchy village.

On July 6th we returned to Algiers to await transportation to some new field of action. Speculation was rife among the boys as to "what next." Some said we were to go to Texas, to round that state up, others said they wanted us in Mexico. Everyone had a guess, but none knew our destination, only that we were to take ship. We wrote letters to our friends in the North that we were going to some unknown destination, of which they would learn later. On the 21st, orders came to draw 15 days rations, strike tents, pack all our belongings and board the steamship *Arago*. All day we worked loading up, and at eventide two thousand men marched aboard ready to try the great deep on shipboard.

Part Two

On to Washington. An Ocean Voyage. We crossed the
Potomac, joined Sheridan in the Shenandoah Valley—
Winchester—Fisher's Hill and Cedar Creek.

On the 22d day of July the Prow of the *Arago* was turned south and with a silent farewell to our dark eyed French and Spanish girls, we floated down to the mouth of the Father of Waters. Again rumors began to go the rounds and guessing as to our destination was indulged in by many. Pensacola, Key West, Mobile, Galveston, Brownsville, and the Potomac were points named. About 11 o'clock in the forenoon, we struck a bar and were fast aground. Here we remained until noon the next day, when lighters came to our assistance, the troops removed and the ponderous old vessel once more floated.

The troops were again put aboard, pilot dropped and the ships' nose pointed out into the blue waters of the Gulf. Sealed orders were opened by Gen. Grover and our destination announced to be the Potomac. On this announcement one fellow in his exuberant joy yelled, "Glory to God, I am going to get one more drink of good old cold spring water before I die," and another fellow said, "hold on Jim, the *Georgia* is in these waters, she may shoot a hole in our vessel and sink us."

E. E. Blake

"Then by thunder we'll take salt water" said Jim. Anything would be preferable to the rotten, dirty, stinking, dead, oozy slime that has been splashed and mixed by frogs, snakes and alligators, for the past hundred years and dished up to us as water.

As a matter of fact, the regiment had not anticipated such good news. From the time we lay at Helena Ark. praying for active service to the present, we had been constantly on the move in a country containing innumerable swamps and bayous. No live springs of wells of pure water. Our supply both for drinking and cooking purposes being drawn from the swamps and pools that had become stagnant under the burning Southern sun and was not fit for dumb brutes, let alone men who had come from a country abounding in pure and wholesome water. Do you wonder the good news was hailed with shouts of joy by the regiment? We had in mind the bubbling springs and cold mountain streams of the North land, besides we were destined for new fields of action.

For two years we had been reading "all quiet on the Potomac," or "our army has crossed the Rapidan," and the next day it would be, the army was falling back on Washington. We had often wished we might be transferred to Washington, and now to be assured of the coveted change we just went wild with joy.

While we were rejoicing over our good luck, our vessel was pushing out into the blue water, where the waves began to lift up the bow and sink it again to conform to the action of the

THE 28TH IOWA INFANTRY

waves. All at once a quietness seemed to steal over the boys. One would think we were getting ready for a battle, so still was it, while up and down went the old *Arago* passing over the great swells of the old ocean in her course out into the Gulf. Finally the stillness was broken by some poor fellow, whose face had become white from his unearthly sickness and he had decided to unload his seemingly over-filled stomach into the great deep. This he did by laying down on his stomach, putting his pale face over the side of the vessel doubling up in a knot and yelling "New Yorrik," when Pat (the wag of the regiment) would yell out, "We ain't a going to New Yorrik, we are going to the Potomac, you blamed fool," or "hear that now, that fellow has been stuffing himself with half cooked beans again, and he ought to know they would dwell in his stomach," or "arrah there, bejabbers, give the calf more rope," and other expressions of like nature.

If anyone can correctly describe the sensations of a sea sick soul, I would like to have it done. I was sea sick but just thirty minutes, just long enough to cause me to cast up a box of sardines I had eaten and consign them to the elements from whence they had been originally taken. My short experience took place on the bow of the ship as I stood gazing out over the great Gulf of Mexico, when the bow of the ship was lifted up on a great wave. The lifting up did not bother me, but as the ship's bow sunk into the hollow of the waves my poor stomach just seemed to turn inside out, scattering its contents in the waves of the sea, and I learned what sea sickness was, but could not describe it. Just imagine fifteen hundred fellows out of two thousand uniting in one grand "whoop up" of the contents of their seemingly over-burdened gizzards and you will have a faint idea of the condition of the troops on the *Arago*, soon after striking the blue water of the old ocean. Our regiment being quartered on the upper deck fared better than those crowded below in the cabins and steerage.

After we had been out a day or two off the coast of Florida, we noticed the captain of the ship and Gen. Grover planning for some defensive operations. Thirty pound Parrott guns with which the vessel was supplied were gotten into position on the deck and such other arrangements made as to call out inquiries from the boys. We were informed the rebel cruiser *Georgia* had captured and sunk one of our vessels shortly before, and was liable to attack us and if she did, we were to fight her and run. This was a new experience to us land-lubbers, who felt sure if we had them on land we could do them up, but this fighting on water with nothing to stand on but a frail plank did not meet with our approval. However, we were ready to do our part.

The next morning quite early, the look-out at the mast head sang out "a sail ho." Soon off toward the coast loomed up the black hull of a rakish looking craft and the boys said, "*Georgia*, by thunder," but on her nearer approach she run up the stars and stripes, at once relieving us of further anxiety. She proved to be one of our war vessels cruising along the coast looking for blockade runners and the *Georgia*.

THE 28TH IOWA INFANTRY

Our experiences on this trip were not pleasant. It was extremely hot. Water was scarce, a pint each day to a man and that warm, besides the crowded condition of the vessel and the many who were sea sick, all combined to make our condition unpleasant in the extreme. But we were going to Washington and could afford to be patient and forbearing.

On the 1st day of August at 2 a. m., we were startled from our dreams by a voice from a picket boat at the mouth of the Chesapeake Bay saying, "who comes there?" then sang out through the captain's trumpet, "the steamship *Arago* from New Orleans." "Where bound?" "Fortress Monroe." "What's your cargo?" "U. S. troops." At 3 o'clock we anchored off Fortress Monroe.

Here water boats came along side and we were furnished a fresh supply of water and ordered to report at Washington City, Gen. Auger commanding. August 2d we landed at Alexandria where we left the *Arago* and took ferry boats to Washington, going into camp at the Pennsylvania Depot, where we lay until the next day. Oh, what a relief it was to be able to draw a full draught of the pure air of heaven or quench our thirst at the pure fountains that gushed out of the hills in and about the Nation's capital.

Many a fervent "thank God" welled up from our joyous hearts, because of the change from the swamps of the sunscorched South, to the beautiful sun-kissed hills of the northland. No wonder our hearts broke forth in joyful acclamations and meeds of praise.

E. E. Blake

The fame of Iowa troops had preceded us to Washington, their fortitude, coolness and bravery in battle was a matter of history, but up to this time no Iowa regiment had ever entered the city and when it was learned we had arrived, hundreds came to see us, to shake our hands and cheer us by their friendly greetings.

Our representatives in Congress, Senators, and Government officials accompanied by their wives and children came through our camps to bid us welcome and assure us of their sympathy and love. It was amusing to see the boys. They would get their hair cut short, buy a new towel, a cake of what they dubbed "button hole boka soap" and repair to some running brook cold as ice, soap their heads and necks, then souse them into the cold water and rub and scrub until they were red in the face, trying (as they said) to get the filth of the Louisiana swamps off them.

Our clothes were old and worn, our flags tattered and torn. We did not cut a very fine figure alongside of the dandies of Washington, who had done nothing but guard duty. Neither did we compare very well in appearance with the hundred-day's men in and about the city, but when on the 3d we fell into line and marched down Pennsylvania Avenue with our old time proud elastic step, every foot fall in exact time to the beat of the old drum, our old battle scarred banners floating in the breeze, the hundreds who lined the streets felt that with a few such regiments, broken-in members as we were, Early could not take Washington. The public press in Washington and other cities spoke of us in words of praise and commendation for our former service and soldierly deportment, and we, remembering past services, felt a pride in meriting praise from the loyal and true.

On the evening of the third, we went into camp at Ten Alley town [Tenleytown], remaining until the 11th. We then went to Fort Bunker Hill to remove obstructions from its front, returning again to camp.

While here, an effort was made to get the regiment exchanged into some brigade doing guard duty about the capital, but as was the talk at the time, General Sheridan said that he had need for tried and true troops and knowing us to be such, he would rather have us than a whole brigade such as were then guarding about the capital, and our vision of easy times vanished.

On the 14th we took up the line of march out over the Potomac, toward Leesburg, which we reached on the afternoon of the 17th. Here we were ordered to hasten across the mountain and join Sheridan at Berryville. We left at 3 p. m., crossed through Snicker's Gap, waded the Shenandoah River, and at 3 a. m. joined onto the Army of the Shenandoah. We were in the very place we had been hoping to see, and had crossed the "Potomac."

It was here we first saw "Little Phil." He came riding along and asked, "What regiment is this?" When told he said, "Yes, I have heard of you boys. We will have some fighting for you in a few days," and the boys cheered.

E. E. Blake

The army moved back to near Charlestown (where John Brown was hung) and threw up fortifications.

Here we were assigned to the 4th Brigade, composed of the 28th and 24th Iowa, and the 8th and 18th Indiana, commanded by Col. David Shunk. Fifth Division [Second Division], General Grover commanding, 19th A. C., Gen. Emory in command.

On the 22d we fell back to near Harper's Ferry, fortified again, and remained until the 27th, skirmishing daily with Early's army. Again moving forward, we took position in front of Charlestown, singing, "We'll hang Jeff Davis to a sour apple tree" as we marched through the streets, and called to mind the events of but a few years agone. We remained here skirmishing until the 8th of September, when we advanced to near Berryville, where our brigade took an advanced position, holding it against the attack of the enemy.

Early and "Little Phil" had been maneuvering for some time; a hard battle was to be fought. Each was trying to bring off the battle on grounds more favorable to his side, therefore it became a matter of importance to us.

After our brigade had taken their position, the Confederates seemed to be massing in our front. Phil came out, looked the ground over, and went back to his quarters, issuing an order that no one should leave the lines without his gun and plenty of ammunition, and that as many of the boys as wanted to fight the rebel pickets, were at liberty to do so. This, the boys called "Puddin," and the result was, before noon the next day,

THE 28TH IOWA INFANTRY

we had driven the rebel lines half way back to their main body. They were reinforced and we came back in turn. The fighting becoming furious many times. We were often close enough to cuss each other while we fought. One afternoon the Johns sent out a brigade to assist their pickets, and a lively battle was on in no time. Sheridan, hearing the racket, came out on the hill overlooking our line and watched the fight for some time, and finally said, "Go in boys, if you get the whole army into a fight it will suit me, or if you clean Early out, it will save me the trouble."

There were many incidents of personal daring, and what is called "close calls" during these days of hot fighting, on our own hook, that deserve mention. The Confederates occupied a spur of a mountain in our front. They would climb around among the rocks and trees, and when a luckless Blue Coat showed himself on the picket line, ping, would come a minié ball too close for comfort. We resolved one night to drive them out the next day. Our plans were formed, and the next morning many of the regiment were outside the picket line advancing on the Confed's, everybody to approach as best he could the Confederate position, and look out for his head, which was always in danger. In a short time after we began sneaking up toward them, a Johnny hallowed over and said, "Hello Yanks, some of you fellows are going to get killed if you don't look out." Just about this time, one of our boys off to the left got a bead on him and shut off his wind. One of the boys in climbing through a fence, had a ball put through the rail his bread basket lay on. Another had a ball put through his hat, from above him, cutting out a bunch of hair over his ear. Another had the seat of his pants perforated and got the laugh from the Johnnies for jumping.

Hardly a man escaped without some mark of the evidence of their close contact with real live rebels. Those days were spent in continuous warfare, often becoming very warm and spirited affairs, until the 18th.

Gen. Grant having left City Point to visit Sheridan, learning of the position of the rebel army, asked Sheridan if he could move on the Confederates, beat them in battle, and follow up the victory. When answered that he could, Grant said then beat him and do it at once, and on the evening of the 18th we began to move on Early's army posted along the Opequan Creek in a strong position. A field on which our armies had been twice defeated prior to this time.

All night long we were approaching the rebel position, getting our lines formed for a gigantic struggle. The two armies were about equal in numbers, the Confederates had the best of us in position and fought on the defensive. We had to develop their position as we advanced, yet we were going in to win, no matter what the cost and ere the sun's rays had gilded the crest of the mountains on either side of us, our advance had begun, and in a short time the regiment was hotly engaged. The first brigade of our division were in our advance in the beginning of the contest and were forced back through our lines.

THE 28TH IOWA INFANTRY

We steadily advanced, shot, shell and canister, coupled with a murderous fire of rebel infantry, who held a position in the rear of a worm or rail fence in our immediate front, and made our position one of the hottest we had ever occupied. We remained here pouring into the Confederates volley after volley, until the right of the brigade was pressed back, exposing us to a flank fire, when we fell back a short distance to the timber, where we rallied and charged a rebel column then in the act of charging the 1st Maine Battery. Advancing to our former position, we held it until our ammunition was exhausted, then fell back to procure a new supply, other troops taking our places. Having secured a new supply of cartridges we advanced to the front line again and began pouring into them a destructive fire.

At this time one of our batteries galloped into action on our right and began bursting shells into the fence in our front, scattering rails and rebels in a lively manner. Boom, boom went our guns while we were pumping lead as fast as we could load and fire. The Confederates began to waver and the order was, forward boys, and forward we went with a rush and a cheer and the day was won. Away they went out through the cemetery, through Winchester, and away up the valley closely pursued by our victorious troops. Over to the right the 6th Corps was pressing them close, further to the right, our cavalry were coming down over the rebel works charging through their lines and back again, swinging sabers as they went. Crook's 8th Corps on the left were doing heroic work.

E. E. Blake

Thus we pushed their now defeated and fleeing columns down through the cemetery, down through Winchester, we pressed them until night came on, and tired, hungry and thirsty, we halted. The victory was won, a grand victory. Nearly a hundred brave boys who came out of the camp the night before were missing. What of them? Some we knew were dead because while fighting by our side, we had heard the cruel spat of the deadly minié ball and saw our mess-mate go down in death, and his brains scattered over the ground. Again the bursting shell in our lines had taken out a half score of brave boys. We had seen others crawling off the fated field with blood streaming out of death wounds, and the question "how did these brave boys fare?" came pressing upon us. And though tired with weary miles intervening between us and them, we go back over the bloody field, looking among the dead and dying for those we loved as comrades in a common cause.

Who can describe that silent search. Here in the open we find Alfred dead, over there by that fence is Bob, Bill, Tom, and others, there in the hollow is where Jake, Henry, John, and others fell. So we go about under the silent stars, gathering up the brave boys, placing them in narrow silent graves, wrapped in their blankets, then the sods of the valley are rolled upon their silent stiffened forms. This done we turn our steps to the hospital, at Red Bud Mills on Opequan Creek, where hundreds, yes, thousands of our boys in blue lay wounded in every conceivable shape, moaning, groaning, suffering, and dying. What a scene. We find our comrades and

THE 28TH IOWA INFANTRY

comfort them as best we can, then bidding them good bye we return to our regiment, passing over the bloody battlefield again down through Winchester, joining the regiment now ready for an advance in the wake of the defeated rebel army.

Evidences of their haste was made apparent on every side. Broken guns, demolished wagons, overturned ambulances, abandoned cannon, and dead and wounded Confederates were strewn along the way leading up the valley.

"OLD GLORY" AT WINCHESTER
By M. W. Cook, Co. G

In Dixie's land our Hawkeye band then dared
    The hosts of "Southern chivalry;"
Good men and true, and brave ones too, there bared
    Their arms for death or victory,
And sternly fought and nobly wrought
On the storm-swept field of Opequan,
Where Early's hosts rushed madly on
To where we rallied in the wood
    Around "Old Glory" there.

A valiant crew, our comrades who went down
    Before the surging battle's tide;
With patriot's zeal, for country's weal, they wooed
    Grim death as if a bonny bride.
Striving like men those comrades then
"Fought where they fell and fell where they fought,"
Just as loyal soldiers ought
    Around "Old Glory" there.

Like sturdy oak, mid cannon's smoke and flame
    They stood and struggled long;
Heroic lot, they bravely fought, that shame
    Might never mar or still our song;
But every note from comrade's throat

E. E. Blake

Might tell of gallant deeds done then
Where gathered our brave Hawkeye men
    Around "Old Glory" there.

The battle storm still thundered on till prone
    Upon the crimson sod there lay
With gasping breath or cold in death, a hundred
    Gallant boys who led the way,
Or followed near that banner dear
Whose stars through all that lurid day
Shone to guide us on our way
    Beside "Old Glory" there.

We seek not fame but meekly claim a place
    Among the loyal patriots who,
In that wild fray on that wild day, on field
    Where fierce the foe his good blade drew.
With savage yell; and shot and shell,
Like lightning bolts in wanton glee,
Smote comrades as if spire or tree,
    Around "Old Glory" there.

This too we claim, that never shame our record
    Bold and fair and clean shall mar;
Ever we'll strive to keep alive the spirit
    That prevailed in days of yore,
When comrades fell mid shout and yell
On sod red-stained with crimson gore,
Where furious raged the fiery fray
On that eventful autumn day,
When thick as leaves our comrades lay
    Around "Old Glory" there.

(Note: The Twenty-eighth Iowa fought in the "Bloody Angle" at Winchester and lost nearly 100 in killed and wounded. Company G. to which the writer belonged, lost fourteen—five being killed on the field, two mortally wounded, five severely and two slightly—and this out of 33 that were in the engagement.)

THE 28TH IOWA INFANTRY

The first evidence we found that Early ever expected to stop, we got from a little rooster about five years old sitting on a gate post in front of a stone house, who with a comical smile on his little rebel countenance, said to us as we passed, "Early will give you hell when you get to Fisher's Hill. He's going to stop there and shoot you with cannons." We cheered the little fellow for the information and went on hunting for Jubal.

On reaching Strasburg, we found the boy had been correctly informed, for Early's army had taken position on Fisher's Hill, one of the strongest natural positions, made doubly strong by being well fortified. Here he had expected to defeat us, and turn us back down the valley. Sheridan at once began preparations for an attack. Crook's Corps was advanced by the right flank. The 19th A. C. was to attack in front, the 6th Corps on the left. When all was ready the 28th and 22nd Iowa were called out to take the advance and make the charge on Fisher's Hill. Here I append the official report of this engagement as made by Col. Wilson, then in command.

> Headquarters Twenty-eighth Iowa Infantry Volunteers,
> *In the field near Harrisburg, Va., Sept. 27th, 1864.*
> Colonel: In compliance with your request, I submit the following report of the part taken by Twenty-eighth Iowa in the battle of Fisher's Hill on the 22d day of September 1864.
> On the morning of the 22d, we moved forward

toward the enemy a short distance, who were strongly entrenched at Fisher's Hill, a naturally strong position, a short distance above Strasburg. Some considerable maneuvering was made in the early part of the day, but we finally got a position and were ordered to fortify. We had scarcely commenced work when I received orders to report with my regiment to General Grover for special duty. On reporting, I was ordered to the front line, a commanding position from which the enemy's sharp-shooters had just been driven. As a battery immediately preceded me, I supposed that I was there as its support. I soon had constructed a sort of entrenchment, a protection against the bullets of rebel sharp-shooters. Here I remained until about 4 p. m., when I was ordered by General Grover to deploy as skirmishers on the right of the Twenty-second Iowa and to proceed as far as practicable toward the entrenched position of the enemy. We steadily advanced toward their works to within about 300 yards, when, pouring in volley after volley with great rapidity, the enemy seemed to waver, whereupon I ordered a charge. With a prolonged shout, we went after them, scaling their works, driving them in confusion before us, capturing a six-gun battery, a large quantity of ammunition and a number of prisoners. After following them for about a mile, and heavy lines of infantry coming up, I received orders to return for the knapsacks of my regiment, which had been left previous to making the charge.

I have no fault to find with officers or men; all deserve praise; no one flinched or fled, when it seemed we were charging into the very jaws of death.

My loss was extremely light; I lost only five wounded in the charge.

With respect, I am your obedient servant,

B. W. Wilson,
Lieutenant Colonel, Commanding 28th Iowa

Night was now upon us. The rebel army was fleeing before our victorious troops and in order to make the most of our advantage we took up the march, following close after the now twice defeated Johnnies, pressing them so close they had no time for rest or sleep. We reached Woodstock at 3 a. m., and lay down for two hours. With stones for our pillows and the cold ground for our resting place, we were soon fast asleep.

In the early morning, we were up and after them keeping up a running fight all day. Often when reaching the top of some hill we would see the shining bayonets of the rebels' rear guard as they toiled up the slope in our advance.

This was kept up for fifty miles. On the 26th, we fell back to Harrisonburg where we stopped until Oct. 6th, when we began falling back toward Cedar Creek. As soon as we began our march down the valley, a division of rebel cavalry began to annoy us, following close on our rear often charging on our rear guard. This continued until we neared Fisher's Hill. Here Sheridan came back to us, ordered our brigade to form a line across the road and lay down.

My recollection is that Sheridan was mad and indulged in some of his strong epithets in our presence. Anyway he said we were going to have some fun and it would be at the expense of the Confederates. A brigade of cavalry had been sent away around up the valley to the right with orders to fire a barn or mill as a signal they had reached the designated place, then to cross the valley in the rear of our tormentors. The charging columns were formed near to and in front of us. Soon a black column of smoke was seen curling up above the trees, the bugle was sounded and away went the charging column down across the bottom over the stream and up the hill, yank neck and neck with Johnny reb. Soon there rang out the cheer from the boys in the rebel rear, then bang and boom. Soon all was still. In the course of an hour a long line of yellow, between two rows of blue came filing over the hills followed by their artillery and trains. We had gobbled the whole force. We cheered the cavalry as they passed through, and guyed the Johnnies about their running qualities, took the road after them and reached Cedar Creek on the 10th.

This, like all other hard campaigns, left us in a rather sad condition, our clothing when we arrived at Washington was old and worn, we had not had a chance to get a new supply and at this time were almost naked. Many were without shirts others were barefooted, while socks and drawers were all gone, besides our coats and pants hung in shreds. In many instances it was hard to keep the body covered, the air was becoming cold and chilly, especially at night and when the wind blew it blew through more than our whiskers. We were in about the lightest marching order we had ever been and felt it keenly.

On the 14th we were set to Martinsburg on the B. & O. Ry., as guard for a train after supplies. Returning on the evening of the 18th, we lay down in our camps to sleep, little dreaming that on the morrow we would be called on to face death in a storm of shot and shell again. On our return to Cedar Creek, Early had followed us and encamped again on Fisher's Hill about five miles from our lines. He had been furnished with more cannon from Richmond. Two divisions of infantry and one of cavalry had come to his support, and though we had no knowledge of his intentions, he was then making careful preparations for an attack on our lines hoping to surprise us and gain a great victory. While we did not think he would dare attack us after the terrible drubbing we had given him at Winchester and Fisher's Hill, yet we were watching his movements.

Our division had received orders late the evening of the 18th to be in line at 5 o'clock for a reconnaissance in our immediate front in force. We were in line as ordered. The morning was cold and chilly and as we stood shivering in the gray of the early morning one of the boys got mad and swore a blue streak, asserting that there was not a Johnny in forty miles of us and there was no use of our being compelled to get out and stand in line and freeze for nothing. That grumbler came to grief, for inside of an hour he lay near the Winchester Pike wounded and repentant over his hasty words, and to add to his grief and vexation, after the army had fallen back a woman came to him and spit in his face. While he was swearing, boom, boom, and rattle went the cannon and muskets of our enemy right down on our left. Crook's 8th Corps were driven out of their camp back toward us, shot and shell were flying across our flank and we realized at once the 28th would need to keep cool and fight with all their old time bravery and every other regiment with it, if we proved victorious this day.

Our division lay on the left of our corps, our regiment on the left of the division to the right of the pike near Cedar Creek bridge. We were immediately ordered across the pike to a ridge running back of Crook for the purpose of checking the rebel advance and giving him time to rally his forces. We were not aware at this time the rebel lines lapped away around to our left and we were completely enveloped in their fast advancing lines. We were ordered to hold this position which we did until flanked on both sides. The 12th Maine were ordered to form on our right to close up the gap between us and the rest of the division, but after one or two attempts were unsuccessful and fell back, leaving us between the rebel lines, fast closing in on our rear. Our officers seeing our danger ordered us to double quick. For about one third of a mile we retreated passing through between the rebel lines, through a

THE 28TH IOWA INFANTRY

most destructive fire, minié balls falling like hail from both flanks and rear, the regiment kept up a running fire during this terrible ordeal. It was a time to test the bravery of the stoutest heart, but when you see the boys loading their guns as they double quicked along parallel with a line of the enemy on either side and when loaded turn and with steady aim put a shot into an advancing rebel, you could do no less than accord to him a place among the bravest of the brave. It was thus the gallant 28th came out of that desperate position. We left nearly 50 of the brave boys dead and wounded on this bloody spot, our Colonel being wounded but got off the field.

We continued to fall back until we reached Sheridan's headquarters, where we rallied and gave the now victorious foe a few volleys, checking their advance for a moment. The enemy continuing to flank us on the left, the whole army fell back so our left was uncovered from their right giving us an even chance at the rascals.

It was at this point some of the boys became so busily engaged firing into the advancing columns, they did not notice the regiment had fallen back and left them, until one of Co. K, raising up to shoot, was killed and fell onto the writer, as he was kneeling behind the stone wall loading. I looked at the dead comrade, then down the line and for the first time realized that all that remained of our force was the dead and wounded, myself and one other. I spoke to him saying, "Dan we're going to be captured if we remain here." Dan replied, "I will die before I surrender, let us make a run for it," and we started. Poor Dan, he only got a short distance until he was shot and I heard the Johnnies say, "surrender you yankee devil," and casting one glance backward saw Dan standing before a row of bayonets, one hand up, the other hanging by his side with a crimson stream trickling off his fingers Dan was a prisoner.

There was no time for loitering. It was a long run to where our lines had formed, and between me and that line shot, shell, and minié balls were flying thick as hail. What should I do? If I stopped the prison pen and probably starvation was before me; if I went on death seemed certain. I stopped for a moment in a creek and debated the question, then threw down my haversack, pushed my cartridge box well back, dropped my gun to a trail arms and started, slowly at first, until I raised the hill and entered the storm of bullets as they sped on their way, then I just gathered all my energies together and with the speed of a scared hound I flew up that long hill while the whizzing, zipping minié balls seemed to be raining all about me occasionally tearing through my clothing and burning my skin, while the screeching swirling bursting shells made awful music above and around me. But I got there. I had fought, and run away, and lived to fight another day. Reaching the line I laid down to rest by an Indiana regiment and was cheered for the brave run and complimented on my sprinting qualities.

If I could have the sounds I heard that day as I sat on the banks of that little Virginia stream, debating the question whether to remain there and be taken prisoner, go to Libby

THE 28TH IOWA INFANTRY

Prison or Andersonville and starve to death, or make a brave run for life and liberty through that awful storm of shot and shell, set to music, the description of all other battles and marches would be failures compared to it. No man can describe the awful din. The boom and roar of scores of cannons, shrieks and screech of flying shell, whirr of the broken fragments of bursting shell as they went singing through the air, their tones varied by their size and shape, the whiz, screech and scream of what sounded like a million minié balls flying in all directions. The rumble and roar of batteries as they changed position with horses on a dead run. Tramp of infantry, charge of cavalry, cheers of the oncoming foe, yells of defiance, the beat of drums and sound of the bugle all combined to make up a grand and awe inspiring sound.

Could some great composer have caught each tone as I heard it that day and set it to music for use on an instrument, his fame and fortune would have been assured.

I rested by the Indiana regiment a short time, learned where my brigade were taking position on the last line formed on the retreat that day, and soon joined them, glad I did not conclude to go to Richmond. The Confederates came on and were met with sturdy resistance and such determination that their advance was checked.

Sheridan came into the field from Winchester, twenty miles away. The gallant 6th Corps had crossed the valley and held the center. Crook had rallied his forces on the left, the 19th Corps had formed on the right and preparations were made for a final struggle. Torbott's Division of cavalry were on the left, Custer crossed to the right. Sheridan rode along the line telling the boys we would whip them out of their boots and sleep in our old camp that night.

The boys set up a cheer that was taken up and shouted down the line, our cartridge boxes were filled, and then that awful silence that always seemed to precede a battle was felt by all. Then an order came sending Shunk's brigade down the slope to a dry run where we halted and prepared for a charge on the rebel advanced line. Very soon the order came, "forward boys, steady now, hold your fire, it will be bayonets after the first volley," and up the slope we moved under a heavy fire of musketry.

Steadily we advanced, dropping down to let their shells pass, until we reached the hilltop, then halted, poured one deadly volley into their lines, then with a cheer we charged into their lines and breaking them, pressed them down the hill, dropping them as they ran. Off to our left we could see the 6th Corps advancing on the now wavering lines of the enemy, we could hear the shouts coming down the line, it meant victory. Cheer answering cheer, then the bugle sounding the cavalry charge and away off to our right, down at the woods skirting of Cedar Creek, we could see the cavalry forming for a charge around the Confederates' flank, soon the thunder of their horses hoofs was heard as they galloped away across the field down across the creek, down towards Strasburg in the rebels' rear, their sabers gleaming in the sunlight as they swung them over the now demoralized and fleeing foe. The morning's seeming defeat had been turned into a glorious victory.

No man who has not been placed in circumstances similar can in any manner or for a single moment enter into the spirit or meaning of such a grand victory. It was won, we knew it, but we were not done with them yet. We had been forced to fall back because of their flank movement in order to give us a chance to meet their opposing lines, face to face. Our camp had been left in their hands, all we had, save our guns and cartridge boxes they had captured and to soldiers like us, the bare fact that we had been compelled to yield a single foot of ground was galling in the extreme. Now we had turned the tables on them, we were the victors, and back over the same ground we had been pushed under such a galling fire we were pushing them. They had captured what clothing we had left and had put it on. Some had stripped our poor dead and wounded comrades and donned their uniforms so that many times a squad of them would look like union troops, and as we were driving them from one position to another in our continuous charge, some fellow would rush out in front of us and yell, "cease firing, you are killing your own men," only to be met with a volley that laid him low. Their position was becoming desperate. Nothing could stop the mad rush. Batteries were planted on the hilltops and as we continued to advance, shot and shell were hurled through our ranks, the boys swerving right or left to let them pass, or laying down until they passed over, but there was no halting. Soon we came to our old camp, the Johnnies just ahead of us, who, in crossing the bridge over the Cedar Creek, would cast their guns into the water and rush on, only to be met by the cavalry as they came around on their rear with sabers flashing over the poor fellows' luckless heads with a command to surrender or die. If they failed to surrender their hats, they would be opened out on the crown with a swift saber cut.

Thus ended another day of victory, the last great battle for the 28th Regiment. Gathering in our old camp we began to look over the situation. Our camp was all bare, nothing but the stakes over which our tents were stretched remaining. Our clothes were gone, tents gone, grub carried away, no breakfast, no dinner, no supper, nothing to eat nearer than Winchester, no fire to warm by and the night was chilly.

Here we remained about an hour talking over the events of the day and our grand victory, then up and away to the front, out over Cedar Creek to the heights near Strasburg as advanced guards. Here we began gathering up the spoils of battle.

Every little hill top was covered with evergreen brush into which the fleeing Johnnies had fled to escape the cavalry. We would approach one of these, call out, "come out of that Johnny reb or we will fire into you," and would be answered by "hold on, we surrender" and out would march from one to six Confederates.

Abandoned guns, caissons, wagons, and ambulances loaded

with our camp equipage, frying pans, blankets, clothing and occasionally some of our haversacks were found over the hills and in the ravines as they were left by the running foe when pressed by the cavalry in their charge down from the right flank.

We remained here until late at night, when we were relieved by other troops and marched back to the old position to the right of the pike on the hill over Cedar Creek, and with such articles as we had picked up, endeavored to make ourselves comfortable. We laid our weary, hungry bodies down, but not to sleep. It was cold and cheerless, besides thoughts of the battle. The scenes we had passed through and our dead and wounded filled our hearts with sadness, and sleep refused to come to many.

The next morning a detail was made and sent back over the field to collect our dead together and lay them away in a trench by the side of the pike on the field of battle they had watered with their blood. It was a sad sight to see so many of our brave, loved comrades, who had touched elbows for so long in the march, skirmish, and battle, lying on the cold ground in their bloody garments with their dead pale faces turned up toward the blue of heaven. Young men in the prime of life, who had so joyfully left home and friends for the sake of country, now laid low in death away from home and kindred without a kiss from mother's lips, but such were the sad, sad scenes on so many bloody fields.

While the battle was on, we thought not of these things, but when the sounds of battle had died away and all was hushed and still, then it was that our hearts were wrung in pity and sorrowing sympathy. So we laid them away to rest until the final bugle call to life again, and turned away to our duties.

Eighty-seven of our brave boys had gone down in this battle. Our wounded were carried to the hospitals in Winchester for surgical treatment and care. Every member of the regiment may well feel proud of its heroic service on this field of glory. It was one of the first to engage the enemy, and had fought its way out after being almost surrounded, and with a cheer had brought its flag out through a murderous fire, fighting like Trojans as they came loading as they fell back, shooting as they ran, and afterwards (as they had done so many times before) leading the charge that broke the rebel lines and started them on the run, rallying the Union army to sure victory. Cedar creek was our last great battle, the crowning glory of a faithful service.

Her history is written with the blood of her dead and wounded, who went down in the forefront of her many battles, willing sacrifices for country, home, and the old flag. Her name will last while history lasts.

But Cedar Creek did not close the service of the regiment. On the 27th we were ordered to Martinsburg, as guard for a train going after supplies. Now to one not acquainted with the duties of a soldier, guarding a train would seem an easy thing, but to us it meant far more. It meant a march of 20, 25, or 30 miles without sleep or rest, oft times without anything

THE 28TH IOWA INFANTRY

to eat, taxing our powers of endurance to the last extremity. We were destitute of clothing, many of the regiment being almost naked only having a ragged pair of pants and a torn or worn out blouse to cover their naked hides from the chilling blasts of October.

Some were bare foot, tying rags and a part of a pair of shoes over their feet as a protection from the cold and wet, yet with all these trials we took up the march singing, "There's a better day coming, Hallelujah," and arrived at Martinsburg on Nov. 1st, got our supplies and started back to the front. It was on this march as we were passing through Winchester, one of the boys (Jo) thought to have a little fun with a colored woman standing on the street watching us pass. She was a huge creature, would weigh nearly 300 pounds and very strong. Jo saw her standing by the side of the crossing and rushed out saying, "Why here is my long lost mammy, where has you been all dis while?" When he got close enough, that ponderous woman just reached out, gathered him in her great strong arms and pressed him onto her broad bosom with a 200 pound pressure and said, "Why Honey, wher's yo been, I done be looking for you all ober, wha's you been honey, how I lubs you, bless de Lawd, I'se got yo agin an I'll kiss you," and poor Jo wilted. The boys cheered and yelled, "Kiss him Dinah, kiss yo boy." Jo never bothered a colored woman again, he had learned his lesson.

That night we got into camp quite late. After we had gathered the top rails off a fence, built our fire and laid down to rest, we heard a belated traveler yelling, "Pheres Co. G?"

Someone in one of the companies said, What regiment? "Ony bloody regiment," he yelled, "Oi am don up ye bet yer loif and lay me doon, I must or I'll die be jabbers," and down he laid him with Co. G.

The next day we arrived at the front (Cedar Creek) unloaded our supplies and returned to Martinsburg. Where we remained until after election, casting our votes for president and vice president resulting in 295 for Lincoln and 34 for McClellan. It was a bitter pill for us to know 34 of the old battle scarred regiment voted for a man nominated on a platform declaring the war a failure at the only time in the progress of the war that we could count on success as a surety. Cease hostilities then! Enter into a compromise then! Make a cowardly surrender, of all we had gained in four year's awful war! It was too much for us, and had we known who those 34 were, no doubt they would have been asked to be mustered out.

On the following morning, we moved back to Winchester, remaining here overnight without fires, or wood to make them with, suffering intensely from the cold. The north wind came sweeping over the mountains and many of the boys were thinly clad, and it just seemed to blow clear through a fellow.

The next day we advanced up the valley meeting the army falling back, pursued by a force of rebs, who were keeping up quite a brisk fire on our troops which was returned with interest. Cannonading was kept up all day. Our army had

THE 28TH IOWA INFANTRY

taken a position and were waiting for the enemy to attack us. On the 11th there was continuous skirmishing. On the 12th it became quite general and we thought another hot contest for supremacy in the valley was sure to take place. Gen. Grover wishing to send a regiment to an advanced position one fourth of a mile in front, directed Gen. Washburn to send the 28th Iowa.

In obedience to this order we moved forward under a sharp fire from the enemy and secured a commanding position which we proceeded to fortify.

Working all night we built quite a respectable redoubt and were ready for the enemy's advance, but they failed to come and after a further sharp engagement with the cavalry, and losing two pieces of artillery and a number of prisoners they withdrew. Here we began winter quarters, the weather had become so cold we could no longer stand it in the open field, and "Shiebangs" were the order of the day. Logs were cut and carried up from the hollows along Opaquan Creek, split, notched and laid up cabin fashion, chinked and daubed with Virginia mud, sticks and stones built in one end for a fire place and chimney, or "dog" tents stretched over the top and all was done. Into these rude huts we went four in a mess, and with plenty of wood could defy the cold.

Our camp was named Camp Russell and was laid off in streets, evergreen trees stuck in the ground in rows up and down the street, everything cleaned up in shape and presenting a very home like appearance.

E. E. Blake

We went in winter quarters and felt that possibly we would rest awhile. Our duties here consisted in picket duty and an occasional trip to Martinsburg after rations. There was considerable talk of a raid on our picket lines by Col. Mosby, that noted rebel leader, but he never came in gunshot of the boys. One night the Col. of an Eastern regiment was officer of the day and had (as was customary) to go around the picket lines during the night. He said it had been stated that the western troops did not fear the devil, and he proposed to disguise himself as the rebel Mosby, and capture a post of western boys. He was advised to let the job out, but would not be persuaded it would be dangerous, asserting that when he said, "I am Col. Mosby, surrender," they would just drop their guns and call for quarter and he would march them in and prove his point. And the blamed old fool actually tried it, but when he rushed onto that post and yelled, "surrender, I am Col. Mosby," he was covered with cocked muskets and ordered to get off his horse and surrender himself and they took him in. No use, the boys never surrendered without a fight. One of the boys said the next day, that if it had been the devil himself he would have had to climb down.

On the 5th the brave old 6th Corps went back to Grant at Richmond. On the 9th, it snowed about six inches covering the valley and the mountains on either side of us with its white mantle. The weather became extremely cold, causing a great deal of suffering to those who had to go out on the picket lines.

THE 28TH IOWA INFANTRY

On the 19th, the gallant little 8th Corps left us and we began to think we would be fixtures of the valley for the winter, but on the 29th our orders to march came, and we left our Camp Russell and warm winter quarters for a new camp at Stephen's Depot near Harper's Ferry, where we could receive our supplies right from the cars. We reached this point late at night and lay down on the cold ground to sleep, covered over with our blankets. On awakening in the early morning we found ourselves covered over with six inches of snow.

The weather became extremely cold and our condition was anything but a pleasant one, we had no shelter of any kind, and the cold blasts from the north chilled our very bones. Quarters we must have or freeze, so at it we went, one cutting timber another laying up the cabin while one heated water and mixed mud and another with hands and paddle daubed up the cracks and plastered the chimney, and by evening of the second day we had the roof on, a rousing fire sending sparks up the stick chimney, while we, sitting back before the blazing logs, discussed the question, "Will we lay here all winter, or be sent to some other point?"

On the 31st day of December, we were changed to the 2d Brigade, Brig. Gen. Mullenux [Colonel Edward L. Molineux] commanding, and the next morning entered on the duties of the new year 1865. The Shenandoah Campaign under Sheridan had passed into history. The regiment had come from the south after its services in that department were no longer needed. They had entered this campaign as new troops from other fields, taken up their full share of its duties with their old time spirit of patriotism and had written their name high up on the scroll of honor.

Their bravery in the most trying circumstances had been published all over the North. Our gallant foes had learned when opposing them, they were opposing men who would stand amid the storms of shot and shell, and never leave a position until ordered to leave it, and when ordered to take a position they may as well yield it. And now though established in winter quarters, the question "where next" was the all absorbing question.

Occasionally we captured a Richmond paper and learned through it that Jeff Davis was telling his deluded subjects that England would soon recognize the Southern Confederacy, that soon 100,000 brave copperheads from the North would be marching in our rear. That the Confederates must die in the last ditch if need be, to prolong the struggle until England or the copperheads materialized, in order to keep up their failing courage.

We knew England dare not openly aid the South; we knew those cowardly things called copperheads dare not attempt to organize. We knew that if England attempted a diversion in favor of the South, Russia would have given her business at home. Or if she did not, the army then in the field could whip the South, the copperheads (all that would enlist) and England combined. So the only question that came up was "where next." Our choice was Richmond. We had chased the phantom for more than eight thousand miles. We wanted to be in at the death of the squirming, writhing thing called treason, and it would have been a glorious ending to a long and faithful service to have been permitted to stand by the dying gasping last hours of the gigantic attempt made by the South, aided by the copperheads of the North and England to overthrow the Union of these states and establish an oligarchy on the basis of human slavery in one half of this land, but this was not to be.

Part Three

Another Ocean Voyage
To Meet Sherman.
Savannah – New Bern – Augusta – Sunny South.

Sherman was marching from "Atlanta to the Sea" and some division must go around the coast and meet him. That duty fell on a part of the 19th Army Corps. So when orders came to take cars for Baltimore, we left our warm winter quarters, boarded the cars, bid farewell to the familiar scenes in the Shenandoah Valley, and in due time landed in the fair famed city and took quarters in barracks near the Baltimore and Ohio Railway depot, remaining here for some days awaiting ships to carry us to Ft. Monroe. A ship was soon secured and we were ordered to march down to the wharf. This march through the city was through Baltimore Street. We were preceded by the 13th Connecticut Infantry, whose brass band played a tune which the boys dubbed "Pretty little girl and a hog eye" (whatever that was).

The members of the regiment will always remember that march with pleasure. The windows of the residences along the way were filled with more handsome women and girls and different colored "pups" (Poodles colored all shades of the rain-bow) than any street we had ever passed through, and the "boys" did some lively flirting as we passed along, sometimes getting a smile from some dear one – more often a frown. It was a triumphant march. Our fellows were braced up for the occasion, having in mind the passage of the 6th Massachusetts in 1861. We took a steamer late in the day for Fortress Monroe, arriving there in the early morning, were transferred to a larger vessel, and were out on the old ocean on our way to Savannah, Georgia, to meet Sherman. The trip was without incident, save the passage around Cape Hatteras, which stirred up the stomachs of the boys to a lively activity; something like the experiences on the *Arago* on our trip from New Orleans to Washington the last of July, six months before.

On the 18th of February, we arrived off the mouth of the Savannah River. Laid here until morning, then proceeded up the river to the beautiful city, arriving there on the 19th of February, 1865. We marched off the ships, and up the streets, feeling that we had entered an Eden. Mocking birds were singing, flowers blooming, and the change from the frozen North, to the warm sunny South was hailed with delight, until the question of "swamp water" came up. To students of history – those interested in the history of our own America – it opened up a field for exploration and investigation. Savannah was one of the oldest Southern cities. Here Marion the Swamp Fox fought the British. Here Pulaski the Pole fell in defense of Savannah. Shed his blood for American independence. It was near here at the historical spring, Sergeant

THE 28TH IOWA INFANTRY

Jasper and his fellow prisoners had while his British guard were drinking, seized their guns, shot down the guards, and compelled the balance of the squad to surrender. It was here the Wesley's, the founders of Methodism, had established their first church in the new world, so that to those of us who were lineal descendants of revolutionary sires, who had so bravely fought for American Independence, this spot was of historical interest.

With what pleasure we stood at the base of the monument erected by a grateful people to the memory of the heroic Pole, Pulaski, and called to mind the record of his death as written on the pages of American history. With what satisfaction we stooped and quaffed our thirst at the same old spring by whose brink Jasper spilt the blood of the British guard, that America might be free.

How our hearts thrilled with patriotic ardor when we called to mind that in and around this city, Marion and Sumter had, by day and by night, fought, eluded, and fought again, British and Tories in Revolutionary times for American independence.

We called to mind the fact that our forefathers had fought to establish the Union, and that we had been called upon to perpetuate that union by removing from our body politic that dark stain, human slavery, the cause of the war between the states, and of establishing the Union on a better foundation, that of universal freedom for all men without regard to race, color, or creed. We realized we were, by our sacrifices, correcting the great mistake made by the men who, making our laws, permitted human slavery to be incorporated into the Constitution. But to return to our story.

The duties devolving on us here were to guard the city, and receive and forward supplies to Sherman's army on the move between Savannah and some points east along the coast. No one knew where that lightning of his was liable to strike.

Gen. Emory assumed command. A provost marshal was appointed, who called for a detail as city and wharf guards and detectives, the 28th furnishing her quota.

It was the writer's good fortune to be placed in a position of examiner of passports, and to see that no one violated the revenue laws, or landed any contraband goods.

When a vessel arrived, it was his duty to board her and examine her bills of lading, and see that everything was in accordance with instructions governing blockaded ports. All baggage had to have a government stamp or permit of entry to the Port of Savannah. Blockade runners with contraband goods from England were to be looked after in an especial manner. Guards were stationed along the wharf, with special instructions to look out for these crafts. One morning early, the guard saw a long, low, rakish looking craft rounding a bend in the river below the city, and was at once on the lookout for fun. The vessel came sneaking in thinking she had run the blockade, and was safe in a Confederate port, where she could exchange her $40,000 cargo for southern cotton, and sneak out again, but instead, ran her old brown

THE 28TH IOWA INFANTRY

nose right into Uncle Sam's clutches, and was soon a prize. We got the hauser, and tied her up before the commander of the revenue cutter could board her, making her a prize to her crew, and held our claim for the government over the revenue cutter.

She proved to be one of the bold swift blockade runners, formerly the steamer *Hope*, of Liverpool, England. The captain of that ship, realizing his sad predicament, offered the magnificent sum of $5000 in greenbacks for permission to unload his cargo and cart it up into the city between ten o'clock at night, and four o'clock the next morning, and that fool boy did not take it. What became of it I can never tell. I know I got a pair of calf skin boots, and a bottle wine, and some rooster stole them away from me. I have always thought that $5,000 would have heeled me instead of someone else, who got the whole thing, for I don't think that uncle Samuel ever got one farthing out of that whole cargo. If he did, he never reported it to me, and he ought to have done so to keep things straight. But there was some crookedness in the army and I am not supposed to tell only on the members of the 28th.

Our offices were in a large brick at the foot of Bull Street. The guard's quarters were one floor above, reached by a broad stairway. One day one of the boys belonging to a New York regiment, went out on a pass and by some means procured enough whiskey to get gloriously drunk and came back with his legs warping around each other and undertook to climb the stairs to his quarters, he got to the top step then concluded he had gone far enough, so he just doubled himself all up and rolled back down. Two of his comrades hearing the racket came down and examined him. They looked him over and one says, "Phat the divils de matter wid him any way," and the other (after taking a sniff of his breath) says, "Its drunk he is, the spalpeen" and then he took another smell of his whisky laden breath and raised up and said, "Be the powers I'd give me last dollar to have the half that's in him out agin, so I cood put it in me own stomach," but not being able to pump it out they gathered the boy up and carried him up and laid him away to awake in the morning, which he did for a wonder.

I cannot tell all that happened during our three years' service. It would not do. Some of the boys may be alive yet and have wives and children to haul them over the dead embers of the past, if by any chance I told a joke on them, or that they sought pleasure and solace from the cares of life in the society of those beautiful fascinating southern bells. So what I write of enjoyment with the girls of Sunny South only refers to the single fellows, who were free to dance and flirt to their hearts' content, with no grim female to call a halt. Our Provost Marshal was a "broth" of a boy. He was pining for an entree into Southern society, so one day he said to the writer, "Eph, you go and procure a good hall, make arrangements for a 12 o'clock supper, and get out tickets for 75 good young yanks and as many Confederates as are willing to come (playing them for the girls, you see) and get everything in readiness and we will have a nice time and get acquainted with some of these little female rebels, if they will come."

"Remember," he said, "no man can enter the hall or stay about it, unless he brings a lady partner, and I will have a guard there that will enforce the orders too." So away I went, procured the dining room of the Pulaski House, made my arrangements for supper, issued the invitations, then hurried off down Wittaker Street to engage my girl for the society ball, made the "riffle," and was happy as a clam.

One young fellow in the regiment after getting his invitation hunted among his new made friends for a fair partner, having found a fair young Mary to his liking, who was willing to dance under the stars and stripes with a bold yank in blue, began his preparations for the grand event by careful inventory of his wearing apparel, and a general overhauling and brushing of his scanty wardrobe. When the happy evening arrived he brushed his cow hide shoes, put on a paper collar and hied him down the street after Mary. He found her ready, dressed in her very best, a little out of style yet presentable, but wearing a frown on her otherwise pleasing countenance, and when asked the cause she said, "I am madder than a hornet, don't you think my Aunt St. John is here and she says I cannot go to the ball with a hated Yankee without a chaperon and she must be the chaperon." About this time Aunt St. John came sailing into the room and that boy's heart began to drop down at sight of her. She was about six feet tall, slim as a rail, with a nose like a parrot, gimlet eyes, cork screw curls, and a voice like the wail of a thunder pumper. "Jerusalem, thought the poor fellow, can I face the music before all the boys with that on my arm, and a mild protest was offered, but it was no go. Aunt St. John must go or Mary must stay at home. The poor fellow was forced to accept the arrangements in order to have a partner at the ball.

When they arrived at the ball, laid off their wraps and hats, they walked in from a side door, Aunt St. John looked up and seeing the hall was festooned with stars and stripes, she gave her forty-year-old snout a tilt upwards, hitched up her suspenders and with a voice cracked and full of contempt said, "Well if I had known you were going to have the hated Yankee flag hung up, I would have worn a little rebel flag in my hair." "Well, madam," said her escort, "if you had, I should have climbed up and remove it." "Climbed up, climbed up," she said. "What would you have climbed up." "I would climb anything to remove a rebel flag said he, that is a part of my business," and the fight was over.

So we danced and talked, enjoying ourselves with sisters of the boys we had so recently fought in the Shenandoah Valley, notably a Georgia regiment made up in Savannah, until the morning hours, then escorted our fair partners home and went to our quarters well pleased with our first attempt at making the acquaintance of the belles of the queen city of the South.

THE 28TH IOWA INFANTRY

For almost three years the regiment had been deprived of the refining influence of the society of women and to spend an evening among those whose silvery laugh, pleasant conversation and merry jest reminded us of our loved mothers, sisters, and sweethearts in the far away north land was a change that gave great enjoyment to the single fellows in the regiment, and they were the great majority. Some of the sober minded married men were even tempted to amuse themselves gaily chatting with the girls of the South. I think now of one who fixed himself up in fine style and attended a ball for a few short hours as a wall flower, so he might hear the gentle voices of beautiful women, so like his own that was watching and waiting for him in the far off home in the North. So intent was he to appear gay in the presence of the ladies, he borrowed a beautiful pin of one of the regiment to wear over his manly heart and lost it as he whirled a saucy rebel girl in the giddy dance.

It was reported the rebel gunboat, *Jefferson Davis*, was on her way from Augusta, coming down the Savannah river to bombard us, and we were on the lookout for any indications of her approach. One morning we saw smoke up the river and began to think we would have a brush.

The *Pontiac*, a double ender, lay in the harbor all ready for a bout with her, her decks were cleared for action, all hands called on deck, and preparations made to give the *Davis* battle. Soon we saw a vessel rounding a bend, and the *Pontiac* let loose a shell across her bow, which caused her to heave to, and run up a white flag. It proved to be a river boat coming in on a peaceful mission, and our visions of a naval battle were over.

Some days later, a squad of the regiment went over into South Carolina to hunt ducks in the rice fields. They saw a flock of ducks, got into a muddy ditch, and crawled up in range and blazed away, and kept blazing away, until their ammunition was about used up, without downing a bird, or even scaring them out of the water. Finally the concluded to investigate, and found the nicest lot of decoys you could imagine. If you were to meet one of those same fellows today and yell decoy at him, he would sneak off. They were the wettest, most woebegone, bedraggled lot of duck hunters I ever saw. All on account of a few decoys.

A few days after, an old woman in a spirit of revenge, set a building on fire in the northwest part of the city, and started a blaze that threatened destruction to the whole city. Their fire brigade were colored men and boys; their engines old, dilapidated hand affairs, their water supply came from the water tower near the fire, and near it was to the old Rebel arsenal full of loaded guns, fixed shell of all sizes, torpedoes etc., and quantities of powder, toward which the fire was spreading. The negro fireman worked well enough until it became certain this arsenal was doomed, then they began to drop out and leave the engines. Then it was our brigade was called out for a new duty; that of pressing negroes into service. We soon had a thousand husky fellows penned in by bayonets, manning the engines. As soon as one squad was tired, another

THE 28TH IOWA INFANTRY

relieved them until the arsenal began to burn and the shells began to burst, and guns go off, then the negroes tried to go off too, but we held them fast and compelled them to pump at the point of the bayonet. It was just a thrill – dangerous, because of the explosions, and those darkeys thought that every moment would be their last. Shells began bursting at 8 o'clock in the evening, and continued until 10 o'clock the next day. Pieces of shell and minié balls went whizzing over the city in all directions, yet I do not remember of any serious results to anyone. Large pieces fell over in the bay, driving the shipping out of the harbor. After eight blocks had burned the fire was checked, and our duties over.

Some fool Confederates who thought by burning the city they could compel us to leave, set it on fire in many places afterwards, but they were finally captured and jailed, their devilish work stopped, and the city left in peace and quiet.

But Sherman was moving east at a rapid gait, and it became necessary to change his base of supplies, and we were to be transferred east along the coast to some other point, so boarded the ship *Fannie* and proceeded to the mouth of the Cape Fear River, arriving there late in the evening.

A great storm was coming up out at sea, making it necessary to either put out to sea again or make the harbor. No pilot coming in answer to our signal, the captain concluded to make the trial himself, made the attempt, missed the channel, and went out into the breakers with a grind, rumble, and crash that shook us up in a lively manner. As each great wave came, the ship was lifted up, and carried a little further inshore, and east down on the sand with a fearful jolt. The wind was blowing from sea to shore, increasing in violence every moment.

Thunder roaring, lightning flashing, captain yelling and swearing through his trumpet, waves lashing the shore and receding again. While hanging on to ropes to keep from being hurled into the sea, we were wondering whether or not we had escaped death on the battlefield to be drowned like rats. I remember standing on the deck holding onto the handle of a door and looking out over the seething, boiling waste of water, toward the shore, and noting the wrecks of other vessels, which had been broken up on these same breakers, and wondering if it would be possible to reach the shore, should our vessel go to pieces as we expected it would. Our situation was becoming desperate. It was finally decided to try to land by the aid of small boats, and we were ordered to strip for swimming, should the boat be swamped. But on lowering the boats, it was found they could not be kept afloat and the attempt abandoned. So realizing our desperate condition, we began forming plans for escape when the ship should break, as we believed it must. It was an awful scene. Men who had faced the cannon's mouth lost their nerve when it became apparent we were liable to become food for the sharks, and quailed before the awful storm, giving up all hope of seeing home and friends again.

The tide saved us. It came rushing in ahead of the storm and the ship floated. We got over the bar into the channel, and up the river, and around the bend, into a safe harbor, just in time to escape certain destruction. Had we been in the old position on the breakers, when the worst came the ship would not have lasted twenty minutes, and most, if not all the regiment would have surely perished in the mad waves.

The next morning we put out to sea again, and late at night stood off the mouth of the Neuse River, waiting for daylight and a pilot. Soon after sunrise, a pilot boarded, and we were soon unloading at Morehead City, where we took cars for Newbern some distance up the river, at the junction of the Trent.

Here we spent the time forwarding supplies to Sherman, and guarding the city, some of the regiment manning the numerous forts. There was nothing of especial interest occurred here, except once it was reported the Confederates were threatening Kingstone some distance above us, and between us and Sherman. A force was sent out to look for trouble, and made quite a trip up the Neuse River, but found no rebels. They were charged on however, and while none of them were killed or wounded, the whole command was scared worse than they had been for many days. They had halted and laid down by the roadside to rest. Between them and the river there was an old field grown up with weeds, which were dead and dry and about five feet high. Below the field, along the banks of the river about fifty William goats were feeding. These goats concluded to have a little fun all by themselves, so they spread out and started on a run toward the road and troops, through this field of dry weeds, setting up a bip, bip, baa, every jump, and it seems each goat trying to make the most noise with his mouth.

When the racket began, the captains yelled, fall in! fall in! fall in! And each man was into line and ready to welcome the daring foe with a volley and die, if need be. So they stood awaiting the terrible onslaught, when out trooped the army of goats. A bloodless field was this. Had the 29th Wisconsin been there, no doubt blood would have been shed. But it would have been the blood of goats.

Supplies were forwarded to Sherman's army by cars, which on the return trip brought back many refugees from the interior of North Carolina. Here we got to see some of those long, lank, yellow "poor white trash" that were called "clay eaters." Newbern was overrun with colored people. It was estimated there were 75,000 of them there at the time, living in shanties about the town, being fed by the government.

From Newbern we returned to Morehead City, and went into camp along the bay. The boys busied themselves "Picking up shells from the seashore." They would go out in boats, and gather the live shellfish as the tide went out and bring them back by the bushel, pile them up behind their tent, expecting to care for them in the morning, when lo and behold! They would all come out of their shells, and march off through the sand to salt water again, leaving nothing but a trail in the sand behind them.

THE 28TH IOWA INFANTRY

It was here the glad news of Lee's surrender reached us. We were apprised of something unusual going on by the booming of cannon along the coast. When we got the news you can imagine our joy. Every man went wild, hats were slung into the air, cheers and shouts were ringing from every throat, meetings were organized and speeches made until we had exhausted ourselves. Why, the war was over, we could soon go home. It was a joyous, happy time, but our joy was to be turned to mourning a few days later. Flags were dropped to half-mast, and with blanched faces it was told about in whispers. Lincoln was assassinated, our beloved Lincoln. Tears of sorrow coursed down many a brave man's cheek. How anxious we were then. We could not sleep or rest until the facts both as to Lee's surrender and Lincoln's assassination were known.

Finally a vessel came in bringing papers with full reports, and we knew the awful truth. How sad the intelligence was to us who had loved him only as a soldier could love our great commander.

From here we returned to Savannah where we remained a few days, then took up the march for Augusta, a beautiful city on the banks of the Savannah river 230 miles north of Savannah. I don't know just why we were ordered here but as near as I can recollect it was to guard the city against pillage by the returning Confederates now released from service by Lee's surrender. On our arrival we found the city full of returning Johnnies who still retained their arms, they knew the war was over and were ready to deliver up their arms and surrender, always saying, "well yanks, we won't give up we were whipped, we were only over-powered." Many expressed themselves as being glad the strife was over and while they still despised a "cussed yank," they treated us fairly well and after a time grew quite friendly.

The citizens, or those that had not been in the army and had never seen a live Yankee before (especially the women and girls) seemed to take great pleasure in conversing with us mudsills as they had been taught to call us. In conversation with a bevy of young ladies one day one of them said she could not understand one thing, that all the young men she had become acquainted with in the different regiments seemed like polished, educated gentlemen and she as well as all the ladies of the South, had supposed they were uncouth in manner, ungainly in appearance, and anything but gentlemen, something like the poor white trash of the South. They did not seem to understand how a man could work on a farm or in the shop, get an education and be a gentleman. We were a surprise to them in many ways as they learned before we left their fair city. They seemed to take great pleasure in conversing with us on all subjects principally love and war.

We went into camp on Hamburg Hill about a mile from the city over in South Carolina, where we made ourselves as comfortable as possible. The boys made frequent trips into the country round about after berries and peaches that grew in great abundance.

One day a couple of the fellows were out about two miles in a patch of blackberries, picking away when someone near

THE 28TH IOWA INFANTRY

them broke the stillness by saying, "Say yanks, would you'ns give we'ns a chaw terbacker" and looking around they were confronted by two young girls in calico dresses, sun bonnets and bare footed, with buckets full of berries. Georgia crackers they were. One of the boys gave them the coveted weed and they were soon chewing away and squirting tobacco juice over the green leaves of the berry patch, happy as clams. As they turned to leave one of them said, "Say yanks you'ns might come and see us, you'ns might, we'ns don't have any beaux now, all the young fellows is in the war. I reckon we'ns'ill treat you'ns nice if you'ns will come, we'ns live right over there."

They thanked them for their kind invitation but the honor was declined. You see the boys stood high in Georgia and were invited out. Just back of our camp lived a man by the name of Butler, who had a large orchard that some of the boys visited occasionally. In addition to his peach orchard, he kept a kennel of savage bloodhounds, 23 in number, that he said he would turn loose on us if we entered his orchard again. We learned these same hounds had been used for catching runaway prisoners, who might escape from the prison pen, formerly located here, that they had often caught and mangled to their death poor starved fellows that could not climb a tree when overtaken by them, that his man Butler had followed the hounds and shot down many of the boys. We resolved these dogs must die and Butler too, if he monkeyed with us.

So we made up a squad from different regiments marched up, surrounded the house and kennel and began the work. In

E. E. Blake

a very short time all the dogs were dead and the squad quietly dispersed. Butler was wroth. He said they were worth $23,000 and the government should pay the claim, and the culprits should be punished for the deed. So down he came bringing his wife and son to identify those who were engaged in the work of death. The regiments were called out (all except the fellows that did the shooting) placed at open order and they started along the line trying to find the boys they wanted. The remarks made by the boys were not very complimentary I can assure you. One would say it will only take 20 feet of rope, another would say one grave will hold the three, and so on until the search was over, and they got into their carriage to leave, then the harness was cut, horses removed, and the angry crowd seized the buggy and started for Hamburg Hill, calculating to run them off the steep hill down into an old brewery 200 feet below and break their necks. But the colonel came and stopped the boys and ordered them to their quarters. Butler was so alarmed he went over to Augusta, gave himself up and was put in jail for safekeeping, where he ought to have remained until Satan called for him. He it was that led the mob in the Hamburg massacre later on when so many colored people were murdered. Soon after this we were transferred to new quarters in the old United States arsenal west of the city, where we enjoyed a pleasant month guarding about the city and courting those beautiful girls that would persist in singing the "Bonnie Blue Flag," though they would admit the old stars and stripes looked the best. So anxious were the people to see a live Yank they would come in from the country for miles, bringing something to sell the boys as an excuse to get into camp.

Many young girls would gather a pail of berries and carry them in to sell the soldiers, some coming for 15 miles. They came by two's and dozens. Many of them very pretty, but oddly dressed.

Dancing parties, balls, and picnics were the order among the single fellows, and many happy hours were spent by the side of some bewitching, saucy, Southern belle. Many fast friendships formed, some love affairs that resulted in union of hearts and hands for life. Many a poor Johnny Reb returning found some bold young Yank had stolen his girl away from him. Those mudsills were getting in their work, and the Confeds had to stand back.

But now we begin to turn our thoughts towards our own loved northland and pine to see loved ones left behind three years ago. The war was practically over and we anxious to close up our service and take ship for home. Soon orders were received to march back to Savannah. We went about the city among our new formed friends bidding them an affectionate farewell, some promising a quick return after their promised brides, others wiping the tears of sorrow from some weeping eyes, then packed our knapsacks and in the early morning filed out of the city and with the old swinging step went down through Waynesboro, passed the old Georgia plantations, and on to Savannah where we began our preparations for our final

E. E. Blake

muster out of the United States service. We were relieved of all duty, our service was over. How impatient the boys became They would hang around the clerks asking how soon will you get done, or thunder, why don't you hurry up, until with the intense heat and their bother it became almost impossible to do anything. But the day came at last, rolls were made out and signed, all reports to the government sent in and we marched before the United States mustering officer, G. W. E. Moriton Capt. 30th Maine, and were formally mustered out on the 31st day of July 1865. The next day we marched aboard ship and were soon passing out toward the old ocean, we stood on the deck as the ship drew away from that fair city and silently bid adieu to it and the many friends we had made while quartered there, not forgetting gaunt St. John and her little rebel flag. Soon the city passed from view and we turned our faces towards the homes we left so long ago.

Landing in Baltimore we drew rations and on Sunday morning August 8th, climbed into box cars and were soon rolling on towards home over the Pennsylvania Central across that loyal old state. Everybody seemed to know we were coming and were out in force at all the stations to see us pass, cheering us as we flew along the road. The ladies and girls brought us baskets of lunch and fruit until we had no need for the rations drawn at Baltimore. At a little station on the mountain where we stopped, an old fellow kept a crossroads tavern, he had his barrel of whisky which he told the boys was all theirs if they wanted it. The 28th like all other regiments had a few in each company that would imbibe occasionally. These fellows filled their canteens and when we got started down the mountain got together in one of the cars and began filling up. Soon "Pat" was dead drunk, and the balance stripped the lad, laid him out on a board, placed lighted candles about him, then turned loose. Soon there was an uproar, and we went to see what they were doing, and in answer to the question they said, "why can't you shee, we are holding a wake. Pat's dead." One of the officers went in and made them dress Pat up again and sober down.

We arrived in Pittsburg late in the evening, and were met at the depot by a committee, headed by a brass band and marched to a large hall where the ladies had prepared a fine supper for us. They knew us and had read of Cedar Creek, and many were the questions we had to answer about cutting our way out in that battle, while waited upon by the ladies and young girls of Pittsburg. They could not do enough for us; we will remember them and their generous, hearty welcome while life shall last. The Pittsburg & Fort Wayne RY had provided us with a train of coaches from this point, supper over and "God bless you's" said to the loyal women of that city, we hear "all aboard for Chicago," and climb on and are soon speeding away through Ohio and Indiana. Reaching Chicago in the night we are transferred to the Rock Island road, reaching Bureau Junction for a late breakfast, meals 50 cents, pay before you eat, and by the time the change is collected and the grub on the table the all aboard is called. We had paid 50 cents for nothing. Not to be outdone or beaten too badly each man took a dish of something, one got the meat, another the potatoes, and so on until the contents of the tables were transferred to the cars. Bonniface protested but we were too much for him and besides it was ours, we had paid for it and got it, could not fool an old soldier like that you know. The balance of the way to Davenport was spent guessing what that hotel keeper's politics were, the majority voting him a Copperhead, an awful charge to bring against a man, but we knew there were some of them in Illinois as well as other states. We had heard of them, their actions had prolonged the war a year, cost the government one thousand million dollars and a hundred thousand brave men, and our love for them was not great.

Home, home in blessed Iowa, and with a long sweet breath of Iowa air and a thank God welling up from grateful hearts we drop down from the cars and set our tired feet on Iowa soil in Davenport, soil we had not touched for three long years. Blessed Iowa, brave little Iowa, what a part she had played in the great rebellion. Her sons had never dishonored the flag. Iowa had written a name high up in the niche of fame by the heroic sacrifices of her noble sons, who were now receiving the homage of a grateful people.

Iowa the loyal, the true, and the brave. We had girdled the Confederacy; we had travelled nearly 10,000 long weary miles. We had hewn our way from Davenport to the Gulf, taken part in all the marches and battles in the move on

THE 28TH IOWA INFANTRY

and capture of Vicksburg and Jackson, led the advance on the Red River Campaign, fighting and skirmishing from Berwick Bay to Sabine Cross Roads and back again nearly six hundred miles. And when our services were no longer needed in the Department of the Gulf, we had been sent east to join Sheridan in the Shenandoah Valley, where for five months we were in the forefront of that gallant army assisting thrice in whipping the old Stonewall Jackson corps on their own ground, on fields they had never yielded to our troops before. And by our fortitude, courage and coolness in the most desperate encounters had won a name and fame that was spoken of all over the North. We had watered the soil of the southland from Helena, Ark., to Harrisburg, Va., with the blood of our brave and true. We had made graves for our dead comrades in nearly forty different burial places. We had seen sicken and die of the many dreaded diseases nearly 300 of our brave loved comrades. Near 300 more had become emaciated by the ravages of disease and their health so impaired they were discharged from the service as unfit for further duty and sent home to linger a few days or weeks, then lie down and die, or creep through life a wreck of their former selves.

More than 60 had fallen dead while bravely fighting by our side in the many battles in which we were engaged. Nearly 300 had gone down on the same fields of carnage, sorely wounded, some to recover, others to suffer for a time in the hospital and die at last.

E. E. Blake

We had taken part in thirteen battles in which cavalry, artillery, and infantry had been engaged, viz: Port Gibson, Edwards Depot, Champion Hill, Vicksburg, and Jackson in Mississippi; Sabin Cross Roads, Cane River, Middle Bayou, Mansura, and Yellow Bayou in Louisiana; Berryville, Winchester, Fisher's Hill, and Cedar Creek, in Virginia; and were ordered by Brevet Major Gen. Grover to inscribe them on our banners as mementoes of our hard-won laurels. We had been hotly engaged in as many more severe conflicts in which but one or two arms of the service were engaged in constant skirmishing for days and weeks in succession. Such were the services and the results of the service of the regiment for three years from August 15, 1862, to August 13, 1865.

We boast not of the valor of the boys of whom we write. Two thousand brave regiments shared our hardships and fought as we fought. Some were longer in the service than we, others may have inscribed more battles on their banners than we did, but no regiment showed more valor or a braver spirit in times of great danger or responded to the call of duty no matter how arduous or dangerous with greater alacrity than did the gallant 28th Iowa. We fear not criticism of this our history, it is but a simple narrative of the duties, travels, marches, skirmishes and battles of a brave regiment in its journey from Iowa City, Iowa, around the Confederacy and back to Davenport, told in the same old swinging gait the writer used as he marched all these weary miles, without

THE 28TH IOWA INFANTRY

any pretention to scholarship or scholastic attainments. No apology is made or will be made, none is needed.

The regiment has a record written in the blood of her fallen heroes, her brave deeds, terrible suffering, her fearful sacrifice of life, her free offering on our country's altar in the darkest hour in the nation's history, and this is our apology.

We present to the present generation and to the generations yet unborn, a nation saved from the mad folly of the slave holding autocracy of the South and its sympathizers in the North. We helped to wipe out from the spirit of the Constitution that stigma on our body politic, human slavery, and made it possible to sing, "'Tis the land of the free and the home of the brave."

The Union was saved, the old flag borne in triumph to the highest pinnacle of a nation's fame and flung to the breezes of heaven, there to float, the proud emblem of freedom, gazed upon by the wondering nations of earth, revered and respected by all.

Our children and they that come after them, as they turn the pages of history in the years to come, long years it may be after the last survivor of the old regiment has answered the last bugle call, will point with pride to the name of grand- or great-grandfather as a hero and a patriot in the great War of the Rebellion. This heritage to them will be of greater value than titled deeds, stocks, and bonds. Our deeds of heroism will live after us and as years come and go adown the ages, our services and sacrifices as told in the pages of this little book will keep our memory fresh in the minds of our descendants forever. God has prepared the verdict. Our deeds are approved.